All about Showing Dogs

Champion Ramacon
Swashbuckler – Best in
Show at Crufts in 1971.
This picture was taken
at his home the day after
he gained the supreme
award – and he was still
alert and showing for
anyone who cared to
look. That's the stuff of
which champions are
made!

All about
Showing Dogs

DAVID CAVILL

PELHAM BOOKS/STEPHEN GREENE PRESS

PELHAM BOOKS/STEPHEN GREENE PRESS

Published by the Penguin Group
27 Wrights Lane, London W8 5TZ, England
Viking Penguin Inc., 40 West 23rd Street, New York 10010, USA
The Stephen Greene Press, Inc., 15 Muzzey Street, Lexington, Massachusetts 02173, USA
Penguin Books Australia Ltd, Ringwood, Victoria, Australia
Penguin Books Canada Ltd, 2801 John Street, Markham, Ontario, Canada L3R 1B4
Penguin Books (NZ) Ltd, 182–190 Wairau Road, Auckland 10, New Zealand

Penguin Books Ltd, Registered Offices: Harmondsworth, Middlesex, England

First published 1984. Reprinted 1989.

Copyright © David Cavill 1984

Made and printed in Great Britain by Butler & Tanner Ltd, Frome and London

ISBN 0 7207 1480 X

A CIP catalogue record for this book is available from the British Library

Contents

Preface

Crufts 1981

I stand beside the ring watching my partner handling a young dog at his third show. I bred him and he was sold as a puppy to a lady who soon afterwards suffered a stroke. I was asked if I would buy him back and, on his return, he looked as if he might have that 'special something' which makes the best show dogs. And he is looking good, very good.

I can see that he stands a very good chance of winning the Open dog class. I have bred many first-prize winners in my breed and a creditable number of Challenge Certificate winners. I should be used to this feeling by now. But I'm not. I can feel the tension beginning inside me as the judge makes his assessment. There are other good dogs in the ring, but I know that mine is a cut above the rest!

The judge decides. He pulls Toby out first and I hear the breath I have been involuntarily holding sigh out between my clenched teeth. But there is only time for a few moments' relaxation before he is back in the centre of the ring for the Challenge.

The winners of the other dog classes are pretty good and the judge gives each of them careful consideration, going over the puppy just as carefully as those from the higher classes. The din of three thousand dogs and twenty thousand people packed into Earls Court for the world's premier dog show fades into the background as the judge picks up that vital green card from the table and takes a final look at the dogs.

He makes up his mind and Toveri Toby (who is to become Champion in just three more shows) wins his first ticket. I shout with excitement. This is ridiculous. It's just a dog, just another dog show, just another Challenge Certificate. What on earth is the attraction of this curious hobby? Why do we spend hours travelling up and down the country to show off our dogs? I hope that the following pages may give you some clues as to the answer and, perhaps, help you to travel successfully within the fascinating world of show dogs.

David Cavill

For my many friends in the world of dogs.
I hope that this book will help others as
much as I have been helped by them.

Introduction

The true psychological nature of the curious bond which undoubtedly exists between Man and dog has been the subject of a great deal of research but has yet to be satisfactorily explained in purely scientific terms. Unlike Descartes, who said 'I think, therefore I am' and based a whole philosophy on this simple and self-evident truth, I am prepared to accept that the relationship exists and to just sit back and enjoy it. In a previous book (*All about the Spitz Breeds*, Pelham Books) I spent some time discussing the development of this relationship with specific reference to the group of dogs defined as the Spitz breeds, but the fact that I do not intend to discuss it at length here makes a specific and important point about *All about Showing Dogs*. What you will not find in these pages is the sort of material that is easily available elsewhere. For instance, many books which purport to be about showing dogs include a complete, and very large, section which reprints the breed standards all of which may be obtained cheaply direct from the Kennel Club. Those from the Kennel Club also have the advantage that they are up-to-date and for this reason I have tried to avoid as much material as possible which changes regularly. These include many of the Kennel Club's rules and regulations, quite a few of which are altered in the space of just one year!

At the same time I intended to write a book which will give guidance for *everyone* who takes part in dog shows. In 1982 the Kennel Club introduced a series of one-day seminars for those involved in running canine associations. I attended one and it was excellent. My only regret was that they had not been considered necessary when my wife and I became responsible for the administration of such associations and of dog shows themselves, for at that stage I would have found the day even more useful. As an exhibitor in the first place and as a breeder, show manager and judge in successive places, my need was for a book which would give me guidance on everything from filling in an entry form properly to the techniques of sorting thousands of them when they arrive on the doorstep prior to a large show. I felt that if everyone involved understood and appreciated what went on in the other sections of the world of dogs then we would all benefit. For example, you may think that filling in an entry form is a straightforward and simple exercise and, of course, it is. But because it seems so simple many exhibitors forget to complete it properly, do not look up the details in the schedule, or simply send it off knowing that they have not completed it properly and thinking that it will not take the Secretary long to add an address or to telephone them if a Champion has been entered in a Graduate class. This may be true for just one entry form but if the work involved is multiplied several hundred times then considerable problems can be caused. For the Championship show which I help to run, two friends come round every evening for ten days and spend four hours just filling in the addresses on entry forms so that exhibitors will receive their passes!

At the other end of the spectrum I often listen to exhibitors, usually fairly new to the world of dogs, discussing the placings of a particular judge and, unfortunately, making it perfectly clear to anyone with some knowledge of the breed in particular or judging in general that they do not appreciate what the judge is trying to do. It is true that a little learning can be dangerous but it is better than no learning at all. I hope that this book will provide a sound foundation on which enthusiasts can build.

The book is divided into sections which, necessarily, overlap at some points. I have tried to reduce any repetition as far as possible but, inevitably, there will be areas occasionally covered twice. In these instances I have tried to ensure that the discussion or problem is looked at from the point of view of that section so that you, as the reader, obtain a different perspective. With luck, this will result in a better understanding of the various aspects that go to make up showing dogs and will lead to better relations within our community.

A recent example of how not to do things was provided by a lady who felt that one of the rings at our Championship show at Hickstead, in Sussex, was too small. She spent a great deal of time persuading an enormous number of people to sign a petition which was sent to the Kennel Club. Now there are plenty of instances where a petition is a good and useful instrument of democracy but had the lady just written to the Secretary pointing out that the ring, although conforming to the regulations laid down by the Kennel Club, was on the small side for the numbers of dogs in that particular breed she would have received a letter in reply thanking her for her interest and her suggestion. Unless there was any particular problem, there is no doubt that the ring for that breed would have been made much larger the following year. As it happened, the Group Steward at the show reported the concern of some exhibitors about the ring at the Committee meeting following the show and, in fact, the decision had already been taken to move the ring to a different position and to enlarge it. The complainant had seen the problem as one which the show society would not appreciate and it had not occurred to her that those running the show were just as anxious as she that the ring should be of a convenient and sensible size. Most committees are composed of people who are themselves exhibitors and it is not a battle between one side and the other.

Those of us in the world of dogs, from the latest recruit to the most senior of judges, are primarily concerned with the presentation and welfare of show dogs. Britain is still regarded as foremost in the world for the overall breeding and exhibition of dogs and, although other countries may present individual breeds to a higher standard, there is no doubt that many of the best dogs are bred and many of the best judges are trained in the United Kingdom. We have a great deal to be proud of and, although we are not without our occasional squabbles, we are all in the business of breeding and showing the very best examples of Man's best friend.

Finally, I must note my sincere thanks to all those who have helped with their advice and suggestions throughout the writing of this book, particularly to Jeannie Hepburn, my secretary, who has managed to translate my scribble into a legible and coherent manuscript.

1 The Background to Dog Shows and Showing Dogs

The vast industry which exists to provide for the needs of dog owners has a highly specialized branch which deals with those of us who are involved in show dogs. I estimate that, at 1982 prices, the turnover of general Championship shows alone is around a million pounds every year – excluding Crufts. If we add to this the activities of the breed and general canine societies (of which there are about one thousand five hundred) with an average turnover of £5000, we are talking of another £7,500,000. Of course, all this excludes the money spent on show and grooming equipment, cost of travelling to shows and, largest of all, the cost of feeding and veterinary care of the dogs themselves.

A proportion of exhibitors are involved in supplying services to the rest of the community, either as breeders or boarding kennel owners, as veterinary surgeons or assistants, and many serve on the committees of breed and general canine societies. Very, very few make their living showing dogs. There is a small number of professional handlers, one or two near-full-time professional judges and one or two whose management of large dog shows is almost a full-time occupation, but for the vast majority of exhibitors, showing dogs is a hobby which costs each one a great deal of money! In 1977 one of the canine journalists estimated that the average cost of making up a Champion was £700 – and do not forget that you have to be a very successful exhibitor to even be in the league of those who can think in terms of making up the next youngster they bring out. Allowing for inflation, the cost must now be approaching £1000.

Why do we do it? Many exhibitors are breeders in a small way and get a small return from breeding the occasional litter. Others are successful enough for their dogs to be in fairly constant demand at stud. There is also a certain degree of status to be gained (admittedly in a fairly small circle) by making up or breeding champions or owning dogs which win regularly. On the other hand, the curious world of show dogs is such that more credit is often given to journalistic or administrative ability than to the more important skills of breeding and showing top-quality dogs. Why on earth do we bother? It is not a question easily answered. Some years ago some friends and I were walking out of

Windsor Show with one VHC (VHC stands for Very Highly Commended but I know at least one who considers it to stand for Very Humble Canine!) card between us. We walked past a cricket oval on which a match was being played. One of our group remarked, 'I've never been able to understand the attraction of cricket, or any other game come to that. You would expect sensible adults to be occupied doing something worthwhile? They could have spent all of today at a dog show!'

When I am asked the question, I have a pat answer I have been giving for years. It came out one day when I wasn't thinking, but it is an excellent example of many a true word being spoken in jest: 'Showing dogs is an exciting and subtle blend of skill, luck and political judgment and never ceases to fascinate me.' The first two, of course, are self-evident, but the last requires some explanation. It is not meant to imply any degree of dishonesty. The world of show dogs has its share of rogues, but there are no more in dogs than in any other activity. Most bad judging is simply that, but, like everything else, you get out of an activity what you put into it and when, as sometimes happens, a judge is not experienced or knowledgeable enough to be able to come to a decision, there is a tendency for personal bias to come into the picture. If you have offended someone or helped them this will, often unconsciously, sway a judge one way or the other. This is not to say that a judge will put a poor dog over a good one – simply that when other things are equal, or nearly so, then the exhibitor with the highest political status (in the widest sense of the word) is more likely to win the prize.

Now there is no need to make a meal of this. Whether it is show dogs or ice skating the same rules apply (how often have you seen the judge of one country show a lower score for the immediate rival of his own competitor?) and, in my view, there is no point in complaining about it – you must accept it as part of the unspoken rules of the game. If you want to avoid this element of human competition you just have to put up with a desert island. Eventually, the best and most determined breeder will rise to the top, but it is a long road and those who have early success in any worthwhile endeavour are usually just lucky. I was. I bought a bitch of excellent quality quite by chance and this goes to test another rule: that the higher up the ladder you start the quicker you reach the top! We will return to this important concept in the section on exhibiting, but for the moment suffice it to say that no one, whatever their status, is likely to win consistently with a dog that is not of the highest quality. We are talking of marginal decisions here and I must re-emphasize that it is an occasional and not a regular occurrence. I do not condone it, in fact I deplore it, but I would not be being realistic if I did not mention it in a book of this nature. Eventually, the world of dogs will have proper procedures for training judges and monitoring their performance but even that will not entirely solve what is a problem of society not a problem just for dog shows. Judging dogs is not a 'first-past-the-post' procedure. It requires skill, patience, experience and knowledge and, even then, the final decision is a matter of opinion – and however experienced *you* are, the judge's opinion may not coincide with your own. In the meantime, if you can't stand the heat, the kitchen is not the place to be.

In the rest of this book I intend, as most books do, to ignore this aspect of showing dogs. Despite what the press, both canine and national, say it is a minor irritant not a major scandal. So having got that out of the way, perhaps we can get back to the reasons why people show dogs at all.

Officially, the idea is to test the quality of dogs being bred against an agreed standard and to select those which are closest to it. In theory, there will be a tendency for those dogs selected to be used for future breeding, so improving the quality of the breed. We shall be discussing exactly what this term 'quality' means later, but I do think we can accept that few people show their dogs for this reason. In the first place the number of people who can win is relatively small. At one of the big championship shows the average chance of winning a Challenge Certificate is 1 in 85. The average chance of even a first prize is about 1 in 7 and, in some breeds, it can be as high as 1 in 20.

I believe that most people start to show dogs because they want to win. They have bought a puppy and in the first flush of enthusiasm they want to show it off. Believing it must be better than all the others, they want to prove it by winning some prizes. Most new exhibitors do not last very long because most of them have other interests to which they are already committed and are successful. They will therefore only continue to show if they have some success or some prospect of success. Two years is about the most for such exhibitors because they do not have the time to build personal relationships with other exhibitors. They will not necessarily lose interest altogether and will probably continue their membership of the breed club or local training class.

A second group are lucky and do have some early success. They usually exhibit for three to five years. Having done quite well they breed a litter or take up another dog and begin to build up personal relationships at their local general canine society and within their breed. Of these some will continue their success. They find they have a flair for exhibiting or breeding and it is from this group that the really successful exhibitors, breeders and judges will come. They are likely to become involved in breed activities outside the shows and in the organization of shows, beginning as one of the important army of stewards and other helpers and, perhaps, rising to administrative office.

Cups are only really appreciated by the owners that win them. Still, they have their uses – if only to allow photographers to take appealing pictures!

In general, the list of exhibitors in any given breed can be divided into two groups: those who were in that list five years ago and, with allowances made for illness and death, will be there in five years time; and those who were not in the list five years ago of which 1 in 10 or so will still be in the list in five years time.

Inevitably, these long-term exhibitors will pick up a high proportion of the prizes at any show, although there are always some exceptions and I know of some exhibitors who have made their first dog into a Champion and others who have retained their enthusiasm for fifteen years or more having never won a Challenge Certificate. Now that's dedication, even if it might appear to some to be misplaced!

The five-year-plus exhibitor, although still understandably concerned with winning, now goes to dog shows for many other reasons. These can include everything from the collection of dog food from the trade stands to helping run shows and meeting friends. A commitment to the world of show dogs has been built up and this is frequently lifelong.

Showing dogs can – and does for many – become a way of life. As you learn more you begin to appreciate the qualities of other breeds. Britain breeds some of the finest dogs in the world and there is great satisfaction in being able to watch and appreciate the very best in any field. The seasoned and experienced exhibitor will often spend a day at a show without a dog, just watching and talking. The more you know the more you appreciate what there is to learn, although in our more rational moments we can see that the appreciation of dogs is just as esoteric as the appreciation of cricket, football or tennis. In the world of show dogs we have the advantage of knowing that we are actively improving and refining a being which has been, and I am sure always will be, of psychological importance to Man as a helper and a companion. You can't say that about football!

The Earliest Shows

By his very nature Man is a competitive animal and there is no doubt that from the very earliest times when dogs were just beginning to be an integral part of Man's society and environment some forms of competition must have been popular. These would not have been very sophisticated and would have been confined to forms of coursing and fighting as both activities would arise naturally from the essential elements of life in those times.

Certainly the development of hunting competition which has led to the Field Trials of today must have begun well before any attempt was made to evaluate dogs in aesthetic terms. What a dog looked like was surely very low on an owner's list of priorities – they were much more likely to want to know how fast, how fierce or how fit he was.

The first records I can find of anything approaching a dog show in the sense that we understand it was in Belgium in the late seventeenth century. Here, shoemakers in the St Gery quarter of Brussels organized a competitive exhibition of Schipperke in 1690. At that time the Spitz, as the dogs were colloquially known, were the housedogs of the Belgians and there was much rivalry between the owners who made elaborate hammered or carved brass collars to show off their dogs. The first recognized association for dog owners appears to have been founded in 1776, but there do not appear to have been competitive beauty shows until well into the next century. During that period 'exhibitions' were held where dogs were displayed, bought and sold and where other forms of 'sporting competitions' were held. These would have included bear and badger baiting, dog fights and – very popular – ratting competitions. Despite the law of 1835 banning such sports, in 1884 an English Toy Terrier called Tiny the Wonder was winning bets for his owner, one Jeremy Shaw (a London publican who later took to organizing more acceptable dog shows) by killing up to two hundred rats in less than one hour!

However, by this time dog shows or 'lead' matches were being organized and credit for the first breed show proper must go to the Pug fraternity for 'A Great Exhibition of the Pugs of all Nations' which was held on 30 May 1850. It was a charity event which actually made a story in the *Illustrated London News*.

The first organized dog show where 'official' judging took place was in Newcastle-Upon-Tyne in 1859. It was confined to 'Pointers' and 'Setters' and three judges were appointed to each breed. Despite this effort at fair play, one of the 'Setter' judges owned the winning Pointer and one of the 'Pointer' judges owned the winning Setter! The following year the Birmingham Dog Show Society held the first 'Exhibition' for all breeds. At this time, of course, there were no catalogues or, indeed, any form of registration of dogs at all so each breed was entered in its own kennel name in the equivalent of the one Open class allowed for each breed.

The Kennel Club

By 1873 showing dogs had become a popular pastime and something had to be done to try to sort out the problems which arose from the fact that so many dogs had the same name and that a number of other 'unscrupulous practices', as one author has described them, were commonplace.

At this time the Member of Parliament for Ettington was S. E. Shirley and he and some friends had run an efficient and successful

Showing dogs is not all hot competition. Here, on the occasion of Bill Siggers' 80th birthday, Joe Braddon shares a joke with Bill and Dora Orpen

show at the Crystal Palace in 1872. After the second show in 1873, it was decided to form a Kennel Club to legislate on canine matters relating to dog shows and to publish a Stud Book. Shirley was the Club's first Chairman and subsequently became its President. By 1904 – a remarkably short time bearing in mind that attempts to organize other, rival national kennel clubs had been made – *the* Kennel Club had established itself as the ruling authority, despite the fact that, until comparatively recently, membership was restricted to less than 300 members.

In the years since its formation the Kennel Club has grown so that it now handles around 200,000 registrations each year and all the accompanying work concerned with the permission and regulations affecting over 4200 dog shows annually. It was the first to be formed and its aims and objectives have been copied the world over. The original ten rules for the running of dog shows now run to two hundred plus pages and the Kennel Club has recently installed a computer.

The Kennel Club comes in for criticism, most of which is unjustified. My experience of the 'official' side of the Club's activities has almost always been excellent and since the establishment of modern administrative techniques efficiency has been much improved. To be honest, the restricted nature of Kennel Club membership does cause a great deal of resentment within the world of dogs. It is seen as undemocratic, for the maximum number of members under the constitution is currently 750 and the number of people seriously showing dogs in the United Kingdom must be well over 50,000 (there are many more who show, of course, but these are usually short-term exhibitors as explained in the introduction). I believe the answer is to allow membership to all those who have bred a Champion dog (or made up three Champions in their ownership bred by others) but as this would automatically exclude a proportion of the current Kennel Club membership, little change can be expected.

On the other hand, the membership of the Kennel Club is not very relevant to the day-to-day running of the organization so, bearing in mind that there must be one accepted authority, things could be a lot worse. As I have indicated, I always find the staff helpful and efficient and it is this side of their activities which actually affects the exhibitor.

Crufts

The Kennel Club also owns and runs Crufts Dog Show and no book on showing dogs would be complete without mentioning the world's premier dog show (of which more later) and its founder Charles Cruft.

Charles Cruft was a born showman. Son of a jeweller, he was a travelling salesman (and a very successful one) for James Spratt who at that time had just begun manufacturing 'dog cakes'. The business took Cruft to the Continent and on one of these visits he was asked to organize a 'Canine Exhibition' in Paris. I sometimes think that in the days of the Common Market we do not have much to thank the French for but it is curious to think that they were responsible for getting Charles Cruft involved in organizing dog shows! The show was a great success and as a result he was asked to repeat the exercise in Britain. Putting his considerable flair for publicity to good use (and making a considerable profit into the bargain) he began to organize the series of dog shows that still bear his name. He introduced many new breeds into the country which were first shown in public at the old Agricultural Hall in Islington where the show was held.

In those days if a show ran for two days your dog had to be there for two days (you were allowed to take your dog out of Crufts show overnight on payment of one guinea deposit, although you only got a Pound back when you returned on the following day!) and many dogs were sent to shows by rail. The boxes were collected by agents of the show management who benched, fed and watered them – compliments of Spratts, of course – and they could be shown too. Afterwards they would be returned to the station and sent home. This practice was not confined to Crufts, of course. I have a catalogue of Southern Counties Show dated 1926. One of the rules states that the show management takes no responsibility for dogs sent by rail, although every care will be taken of them and that owners should ensure that a stout benching chain should accompany each exhibit. Prize money was the same as at Southern Counties today: £2.00, £1.00 and 50p (except in the sponsored classes), but the entry fee was 2s 6d (or 12½p).

Charles Cruft died in 1938, two years after the Jubilee show. His wife ran one further show in 1939 and then the war intervened. In 1942 she passed the show over to the Kennel Club, which ran its first Crufts in 1948 at Olympia.

Some believe that Crufts should be moved out of London and it is true that at Earls Court, the current venue, there are plenty of problems – but could you successfully move Wimbledon or the Chelsea Flower Show? Well, I suppose you could, but Britain is founded on these traditions and Crufts is more than a dog show and should stay in the metropolis. I doubt, too, if visitors would fly in from all over the world to Birmingham. Despite my preface, Crufts is a 'different' dog show. You have to qualify your dog at another championship show to be eligible for entry (although this could now be dropped since the show now takes place over three days, for the qualifier was originally introduced only to limit the number of dogs, not to influence the quality). The vast numbers of the general public generates an air of excitement and expectancy not experienced at any other show and a win at Crufts is held in much higher esteem by the general public and your local newspaper than at any other show.

The Kennel Club Today

The 'official' side of the Kennel Club's activities is controlled by five offices. These are: the Show Department, the Awards Department, the Registration Department, Publications and Crufts. A brief description of each department and its work is given here. The staff at the Kennel Club are paid to serve the needs of show dogs. They have specific jobs, which are defined by the Chief Executive acting on the instructions of the General Committee. (There are other committees, but it is the General Committee which is ultimately responsible.) However, like all of us, they occasionally make mistakes. If you have a grievance there is no point in taking it out on the staff. And make sure that you, at least, are right by completing forms accurately and within the specified time limits. It is sensible, too, to get proof of posting (this is free from your Post Office when you post the letter) and also to clearly address the letter to the correct department. Another tip is to keep the contents of each letter to one subject. If you raise a registration query with an application for a Junior Warrant Certificate and there is a problem with one of them, dealing with the other will be delayed.

PUBLICATIONS DEPARTMENT

Publications in this context cover the whole range of the Kennel Club's output. This includes the breed standards, the set of Kennel Club yearbooks which list general and breed canine societies, Kennel Club rules and regulations and lists of members and associate members. The department's major work is the production of the Kennel Club's monthly journal, the *Kennel Gazette*, which as well as containing articles of general interest is also the magazine in which all official notifications are made. These include the full list of shows which have been authorized (with the exception of exemption shows), Kennel Club official announcements, changes in the rules, regulations or breed standards, publication of requested affixes, judges for shows which have championship status, lists of dogs which have passed the various breed certificate schemes and applications for membership or associate membership of the Kennel Club. Because of its 'official' nature, the *Gazette* must be circulated (free) to all general and breed canine societies, so that their committees may be aware of any changes or alterations in policy. A supplement to the *Kennel Gazette* is also published and this is compiled by the Registration Department. It contains details of all puppies registered at the Kennel Club and changes of name and ownership of registered dogs. It is the task of the Registration Department to keep track of all these records and to ensure that all the details of registered dogs are kept up-to-date.

Dogs are part of the cultural fabric of our society. This may sound highfalutin, but it is true: dogs serve as companions and friends to every section of the population

AWARDS DEPARTMENT

The record of each dog also includes details of its performance in the show ring and these are kept up-to-date by the Awards Department. Not all wins are included, but the important ones (those at championship shows) are all carefully recorded. Each year, the Awards Department collates the outstanding wins (at the moment these are 1st to third prize winners in Limit or Open classes, and the winners of Reserve Challenge Certificates and Challenge Certificates) into a complete record of wins, parentage breeders and owners – the Stud Book. The Stud Book has been published every year since the Kennel Club's inception (although the first few had to be compiled in retrospect so are unlikely to be very accurate) and, with the supplement to the *Kennel Gazette*, it provides the formal records of dog shows in the United Kingdom. All past records have been microfilmed and current records are kept in a computer, which has replaced the hundreds of thousands of cards in the comprehensive card index which the Kennel Club used until recently. To give some idea of the amount of work involved: the Stud Book currently runs to over 900 pages and the Breed Records Supplement, published monthly, contains around 90 closely set A4 pages.

SHOW DEPARTMENT

The co-ordinating body for dog shows is the Show Department, which collates applications for shows, publishes the show calendar, keeps show records and organizes the immense task of checking schedules and entry forms prior to publication, allocates Challenge Certificates to shows and does the work associated with checking the qualifications of judges passed or proposed to approve Challenge Certificates.

CRUFTS

Finally, one department organizes Crufts Dog Show. Only the American Kennel Club's Westminster Show comes close in importance, but when you compare an entry of 3,000 or so at Westminster to around 10,000 at Crufts, this indicates the difference in size and scope. The Crufts Show Department is easily the smallest at the Kennel Club but works full-time, all the year round for the big event at Earls Court in early February each year.

Even this brief summary gives an indication of the complexity of the Kennel Club's organization and do not forget that we have not even touched on the extra load generated by the administration of 350 field and working trials, obedience competitions and the Kennel Club's membership commitments. The problems are not simplified by the necessity for almost continuous consultation with the many committees which have been set up to deal with various aspects of the organization, so that the paid staff can seldom take decisions without reference to the appropriate committee. All this has to be paid for, of course, and revenue is raised by charging owners, breeders, exhibitors and canine societies fees for the various services.

The Kennel Club issues many certificates, record cards and forms. Each of these is dealt with in the appropriate chapter, so details of change of ownership are described in the section which is devoted mostly to exhibitors and the application to run a show in the section concerning the administration of canine societies.

Each year the Kennel Club produces an official record of events, which is published in a section of the Yearbook and in the relevant Stud Book. They also reprint appropriate lists of all members and associates, breed and general canine societies, amendments to the constitution of the Kennel Club and all the rules and regulations. These all change from year to year as there are always alterations and improvements which can be made and lists need to be continuously up-dated.

In the early days, the Kennel Club was just that, a Canine Society with special responsibilities for show and working dogs in the United Kingdom. To fulfil its responsibilities it has had to grow and, although some would argue that its 'exclusive' image still belongs to the past, it is now an extremely complex business which, overall, provides an efficient and necessary service to the world of show dogs.

Structure of the World of Shows

Before going further, it might be helpful to look at the way in which the world of show dogs is put together. Remember, though, that this structure developed slowly over the years and is the result of trial, error and subsequent modification, according to experience and circumstance. Therefore, there are a number of anomalies which are now an integrated part of the system and which it would be difficult to change. Certainly, what seems a good idea to some (the splitting of the Working Group into two because it is so large, for instance) will seem just the opposite to others and, therefore, change comes slowly and often not at all. The argument that 'such and such has always been so and worked – why change it?' is always with us and the Kennel Club often finds it easier and cheaper to make minor amendments rather than going in for a thorough revision. (As I write, the number of Kennel Club committees has been reduced and the structure is now much less unwieldy. Their composition has also been improved, but there is still much to be done.) Bearing in mind that there may be further alterations in the future, let us firstly consider the way in which dogs are grouped.

With over four hundred individual breeds recognized by various national Kennel Clubs around the world, each club autonomous in their own country, it is inevitable that different dogs are grouped in different ways. In Britain about 140 plus different breeds are recognized. Anyone wishing to show a new breed in this country must apply to the Kennel Club for it to be placed on the 'Imported Register'. During this time the dog/s may only be shown in special 'Imported Register Classes'. When the breed has what the Kennel Club considers to be a large enough genetic pool to ensure breeding self-sufficiency it can be listed as a 'Rare Breed'. During this process an interim standard is approved and, when there are enough dogs being shown to justify them, the breed gains 'full listing' by being allocated Challenge Certificates. New breeds are imported by enthusiasts from other countries and acceptance by the Kennel Club is usually straightforward. Occasionally there are problems, usually if the 'breed' in question is not clearly defined. If you imported an Abyssinian Hoghound from

Abyssinia and the Abyssinian Kennel Club recognized it as a breed and had an established standard, the Kennel Club – assuming it had agreements with the Abyssinian Kennel Club – would almost certainly recognize the breed. But if you imported it from Turkey (even if, as a breed, it was well-established), or if our Kennel Club had not established canine diplomatic relations with either or both countries then you would be in for a long and difficult struggle! The Kennel Club offers advice to those wishing to register a new breed and I think it sensible to discuss it with them first. It is an expensive business to bring in what you think is a magnificent or unusual dog and then find that it cannot be shown.

The most usual grouping is that agreed by those countries which are members of the FCI (Fédération Cynologique Internationale), which divides dogs into quite small groups. These include 'Sight Hounds' and 'Spitz' at one end of the range and 'Pastoral' and 'General' at the other. In the United Kingdom our Kennel Club has split those breeds recognized into six groups. These are:

The Hounds: those breeds that chase game (sight hounds) and track game (scent hounds), plus some others which are not so easily classified, such as the Irish Wolfhound and the Finnish Spitz.

Bobby James critically examines the movement of a top winning Saluki in the hound group at Windsor Championship Show

The Gundogs: the most homogeneous group consisting of Pointers, Setters, Spaniels and Retrievers, most of which are breeds that have been specifically developed for use by sportsmen.

The Terriers: very much an English group, having been developed in this country for catching small game and vermin.

The Working Group: easily the biggest group of pastoral, guard dogs and sledge dogs, with one or two extra breeds thrown in for good measure.

The Utility Group: all once members of the Working group which were hived off when it became too big to be manageable. Most belong in the group the Americans call 'Companion Dogs'. Some have working backgrounds but most are larger 'housedogs' and they range from the Keeshond to the Tibetan Spaniel and from the Bulldog to the Standard Poodle. In terms of type it is the most wide-ranging of the groups.

The Toys: these are all breeds, mostly bred down from larger breeds, which have been developed as small house/companion dogs.

A complete list of which breed is in which group is given in the Appendix, which also shows the number of registrations in that breed as a percentage of total registrations at the Kennel Club in 1981.

The groups provide one of the frameworks upon which the world of dogs is structured. Another is provided by the canine societies. These are divided into breed societies and general societies and both have regional or national responsibilities. A small breed will have one, two or more societies which represent its interests. The Kennel Club, as a matter of policy, prefers there to be at least two breed clubs in each breed, so that members dissatisfied with one have an alternative. A society representing a small breed may have members distributed throughout the country, but a larger breed will not only have one or more national breed associations, but a number of regional clubs, such as the Midland or Welsh Abyssinian Hoghound Club.

All breed societies have as their aim the promotion and support of their breed, but the regional ones, in theory, concentrate on their own area. In practice, this cannot be relied upon. The 'senior' breed club, which is often the longest-established, may itself be a regional club, and certainly societies which are allocated Challenge Certificates take their membership from all over the country, even if they only run their shows, say, in Scotland. With only one exception (the Finnish Spitz Club is traditionally allowed to run a show for all the Spitz breeds) breed clubs are confined to running shows for their own breeds only, except, of course, for the anomalies within Poodles, Dachshunds and Chihuahuas.

The general societies are nearly all regional, although there is an important subdivision. There are the 'group' societies, which cater on a regional or national basis for the specific groups as defined by the Kennel Club, plus one or two sub-group societies such as the Pointer and Setter Association. The larger general societies, although bearing regional names, tend to draw their support from throughout the country, although only one, the Ladies Kennel Association, can really be described as a national general canine society. Most general societies see their major role as actually running dog shows and although breed clubs see their shows as an important part of their function, they also see it as part of their activities to 'promote' the breed, usually by publishing related material, such as magazines, simple guides for new owners and more detailed, technical material for breeders and judges.

Both sorts of clubs are an essential element in the world of show dogs – although some would argue that there are too many of both. With over 3000 shows a year, excluding matches, I am inclined to agree, but new societies are being formed all the time and the Kennel Club registers a few every year to join the existing 1500 or so. As well as the general and breed canine societies the Kennel Club also recognizes 700 plus training clubs. They usually serve a very local area and may not run licensed shows. They are canine societies but not show societies.

Each society has its own rules, which must be approved by the Kennel Club. The rules are set out in such a way that only in the last resort does the Kennel Club become involved in the club. The rules must be phrased in a way that allows almost complete autonomy in the day-to-day administration, but they must recognize the rights of the Kennel Club regarding permission for and rules governing any shows that the club may run. Politically, this is an important principle because the Kennel Club can virtually ignore any internal problems within the club while retaining absolute power over any activities which relate to dog shows. Any complaints that exhibitors or members may have about any aspect of the society (unless it relates specifically to the organization or running of a show) can only be dealt with by a special general meeting called by the members within the rules of the club.

I mention this because many members of general or breed canine societies expect the Kennel Club to take up grievances about all sorts of things from compilation of a club's judging list to whether or not a vote was conducted properly. The Kennel Club almost always regards these problems as internal matters and (in my view, quite rightly) is not prepared to interfere, although they may occasionally give informal advice, both to committees and to individual members. Most societies work smoothly year in and year out, but there are inevitably occasions when perfectly legitimate disagreements lead to unpleasantness between one faction and another, so an understanding of how these may be resolved is quite important.

Basically, the club rules must always be properly consulted or adhered to and the Kennel Club will sometimes advise on their interpretation. Serious disagreements can often be resolved by a special general meeting, but this nearly always attracts unwelcome publicity and I believe that most difficulties can be sorted out by sensible negotiation between those concerned. Always remember that if the majority really want something to happen, they have the power because they have the votes. If you are unable to get the backing then you must resign yourself to status quo!

Running a canine society is a demanding job and most of the work falls on the secretary. The larger breed and general societies often give their secretaries (and sometimes the treasurer and show managers) an honorarium because it can be almost a full-time job. Most officers and committee members, however, are involved because they love the world of show dogs. Personally, I think dogs should be fun and can see no pleasure in either running a canine society or judging unless it is enjoyable. The anxiety to get into the centre of the ring is something that has always surprised me and my experience has been that if you are good enough you will get there without pushing, negotiating or treading on anyone. It is true that some seem to do well despite their obvious lack of expertise, but what pleasure can there be in doing anything unless you have the satisfaction of knowing it is being done properly?

In my view, everyone involved with dogs should take an active part in a breed and a general canine society. Our dogs give us a great deal and one way in which we can repay them for their companionship is to be involved in their promotion, both to other enthusiasts and to the general public.

Dog Shows

No dog show may be held without first obtaining permission from the Kennel Club (and paying the appropriate fee). In theory the Kennel Club does not have a monopoly and anyone could run a dog show, but in practice the Kennel Club would withdraw its services of registration and ban an exhibitor from entering any of its shows if they took part in an unlicensed show.

Forms of application can be obtained from the Show Department of the Kennel Club for minor events, but the system for open shows and championship shows is much more complex. The initial application forms appear in the *Kennel Gazette* and these must be completed for the date required and then, when the Show Department has sorted out the show calendar, the appropriate application forms are sent direct to the organizing secretary. With over 3000 licensed shows each year this takes some time and the Kennel Club are now working on the show calendar almost two years ahead.

The following brief summaries do not really do justice to the complexity of dog shows. Each type of show is subject to a set of comprehensive rules and regulations laid down by the Kennel Club as well as their own rules which are laid down by the committee organizing the show. They cover everything from what should be included in the schedule to the circumstances in which exhibitors may be entered in an alternative class. We will have more to say about the rules as they affect the various participants later on, but, for the present, here is a brief show guide.

EXEMPTION SHOWS

Registered canine societies are not allowed to run exemption shows. As the name implies, they are 'exempt' from Kennel Club rules and regulations, except in so far as there is a simple set of rules to prevent them

At an exemption show anything can happen. Here Lady Gloria Cotteslow is trying to discover the dog with the longest tail!

competing with shows licensed by the Kennel Club. An exemption show can have up to four pedigree classes and any number of 'novelty' classes. Cross-bred dogs can be entered in novelty classes. Exemption shows are often held to raise money for charity and many exhibitors use them to help their dogs become accustomed to the show ring, so the quality of some of the exhibits is often higher than you would expect. They are also fun: the classes are usually well-filled, so if you lose your disappointment is shared by the others and if you win it is a considerable achievement. Some exhibitors show almost entirely at exemption shows; they prefer the atmosphere and enjoy the day out. Such shows

A puppy Chow at a Puppy Parade. This kind of unofficial event gives handlers the opportunity to train their dogs before they go to larger shows

are easy to organize and almost always make a reasonable profit. Prizes can usually be begged from local firms in the name of the organization or charity running the show and the only expenses are the Kennel Club licence, ring numbers, rosettes, advertising in the canine press and local papers, prize cards, insurance and a present for the judge. Entries are usually taken on the day during the two hours or so before judging begins. Incidentally, careful records of entrants and prizewinners

FIG. 1   Entry form

ENTRY FORM

OWNERS NAME...

ADDRESS..

....

DOGS NAME......................SEX.............................

Class 1............................

Class 2............................

Class 3............................

Class 4............................

Class A............................

Class B............................ State under 10 ~~or 10 to 15~~

Class C............................

Class D............................

Class E............................

Class F............................

Class G............................

Class H............................

Class I............................

TOTAL ENTRY FEES..

FIG. 2   Record of
entries

NAME OF DOG	RING N°	CLASS													Total Fee
		1	2	3	4	A	B_A	B_B	C	D	E	F	G	H	I	

FIG. 3   Steward's sheet

.... **SHOW**   DATE ....

BREED   ....   **JUDGE** ....

CLASS No.	DESCRIPTION	1st	2nd	3rd	RES.	V.H.C.	H.C.	REMARKS

B.O.B. ....

BEST DOG ....   BEST BITCH ....

RESERVE BEST DOG ....   RESERVE BEST BITCH ....

should be maintained and then kept for a short while. As well as providing extra publicity for the organization running the show by submitting the names of prizewinners to local papers, queries do sometimes arise when an exhibitor needs to be contacted. The three simple forms required for running an exemption show are on pages 22 and 23. They are self-explanatory and will provide all the records you need.

One thing that organizers of exemption shows often forget is to insure themselves against their third party public liability. Most charitable organizations will have a policy which covers this sort of event, but if they have not the organizers should take out a 'special events' cover for the day. Any local insurance broker will be able to do this simply and cheaply.

MATCHES

The Kennel Club lays down comprehensive rules for matches, although they are quite simple. No entry form needs to be completed before the day of the match and they are usually organized between competing teams representing breed or general canine societies. Only registered canine societies are allowed to run or take part in matches and a Kennel Club licence is required. Apart from this, a judge, ring numbers and a rosette or prize for the winner, very little organization is required.

As exhibitors enter their dogs with the secretary or show manager, they are placed in two lists, according to the team they represent, until they are all entered. In general, the number is 32 dogs but it can be more or less, the 'spare' dogs being given a 'bye'. Two numbers are drawn out of a hat (or just from the list) one from each team and the dogs are judged. The winner goes forward into the next round as in a knockout tournament, the one remaining at the end being the winner. Societies will often run two matches in an evening – one for puppies, perhaps, and one for adult dogs.

PRIMARY SHOWS

These shows have only recently been introduced by the Kennel Club and allow societies to hold a very limited number of classes without having to go to the expense of printing a schedule, receiving entries and printing a catalogue in advance. Exhibitors may turn up and enter on the day, in the same way as they can at matches, so apart from advertising (and many societies who put on primary shows do so as part of their normal club activities and so the members usually know anyway), only ring numbers, prize cards and a judge are needed.

Like a match, a primary show is easy to organize, it is an enjoyable social event and gives exhibitors the opportunity to give their dogs practice as well as providing a training ground for judges.

Pamela Cross-Stern examines the puppies at a Spitz Spectacular. Here judging in terms of the rules laid down by the Kennel Club is not taking place and Pamela is assessing the dogs in relation to their potential rather than their merit. This sounds complicated, but it means that groups of exhibitors can have a day out without the pressure of competition

SANCTION SHOWS

These are the first of the shows which fall within the Kennel Club's regulations for licensed shows. The major difference between these shows and the smaller shows is that a schedule of rules, classes and judges must be published (and sent to the Kennel Club), that entries must be received in advance and a catalogue (which must include the names, owners, breeders and breeding of each dog and a list of the classes and the dogs entered in each class) printed. The number of classes at a sanction show is restricted as are the times at which they may be held. This is so that permission for holding them can be given quickly and easily in the knowledge that they are unlikely to clash with larger, more important shows. Entry is also restricted to members of the society holding the show so they remain small, friendly events with the exhibitors usually only coming from the immediate area.

LIMITED SHOWS

As in sanction shows, exhibitors must be members of the club running the event but they are less restricted on the number of classes scheduled and the show may be held at any time. Although most limited shows are quite small, a few have considerable prestige. Some of our major canine societies hold limited shows for their members only and the competition at these events can be very hot.

A popular competition at many dog shows is the Junior Handling. In these classes the ability of the handler is being judged, not the quality of the dog. Here Celia Tomlinson examines a group of youngsters, one of whom appears to be having a little trouble with his Chow

OPEN SHOWS

As the name implies, open shows are open to all exhibitors and any Kennel Club-registered dog. Open shows can be of any size so long as the Kennel Club considers that adequate facilities are available. Breed associations as well as general canine societies may hold open shows and they range from as few as ten to over a thousand classes. One restriction on which the Kennel Club insists is that only the small shows (up to about 200 classes, although a lot depends on past entries and the venue) may be held without benching. Benches are partitioned ranks of low stalls on which dogs can be placed for the duration of the show (except, of course, when they are being judged). Many exhibitors resent benching – particularly as they have to pay the extra costs of having it – but most show managements believe that benching makes a show more cohesive and easier to organize.

(A description of benching, and some other simple terms, may seem superfluous to most readers, but when I went to my very first dog show I thought that the show being 'benched' meant that the exhibitors were given something to sit on to watch the judging and I often meet people with some experience who make statements about dogs and shows which clearly indicate that they do not understand some of the basic concepts.)

The open show is generally regarded as a more serious stage of competition than the other licensed shows. They are an important facet of the world of shows, although they, along with the sanction and limited shows have lost a good deal of ground during the last twenty years as the improvements in our roads have enabled more and more exhibitors to join the championship show circuit. As a result, the numbers of open shows have decreased and the number of entries, overall, has suffered a decline.

CHAMPIONSHIP SHOWS

Each year the Kennel Club fixes the number of Challenge Certificates which will be available for each breed two years hence. The figure is arrived at through a formula which takes into account the number of dogs being shown during the preceding two years. So, the more dogs being shown in a given breed, the more sets of Challenge Certificates will be available in two years' time (except in the very largest breeds). To gain one a dog has to beat all the others of its sex at a show at which Challenge Certificates are available. To become a Champion it then has to gain two more under different judges. CCs, as they are called, or 'tickets' are very, very difficult to come by and it is probably harder to make up a Champion in the United Kingdom than in any other country in the world. The competition is very fierce and that is one of the reasons why Britain breeds some of the very best dogs in the world.

The number of CCs available in each breed is distributed among a number of senior canine societies – the 'general championship shows' – and individual breed clubs where enough are available. The fewest number of CCs to any breed is ten sets, and breeds with insufficient numbers to justify certificates are classified as 'rare' breeds. The three representative shows – the Scottish Kennel Club, the Welsh Kennel Club and Birmingham National Show – plus Crufts are automatically allocated sets of the certificates, the others being distributed as the Kennel Club thinks fit.

The general championship shows number their entries in thousands and most are held over two or three days and, of course, running such a show is almost a full-time job. Some general championship shows (and many open shows) are run by agricultural societies or local town or city authorities. Nevertheless, although they are largely independent of the show and society structure of the Kennel Club, they must still agree to be bound by the Kennel Club rules. Each of the six 'groups' also has a senior society which runs a championship show and many of the senior breed societies are allocated certificates too.

Because these critical green cards (they are not green in fact, but are printed in green ink) are allocated directly by the Kennel Club, they insist that judges entrusted to hand them out must be approved by them and a special committee meets to consider the judges appointed by the societies. Those being asked to give 'tickets' for the first time must complete a special Kennel Club questionnaire, which is reviewed

Exhibitors spend a long time waiting to be judged, especially in the larger breeds. Here the exhibitors of Old English Sheepdogs line up for the judge at Windsor Championship Show in the shadow of Windsor Castle

by the Judges Sub-Committee, who often write to breed clubs to ask for their opinion. It is a complicated and necessary procedure but, because the 'rules' are not very clear, because the committee sits in private (understandably) and because the mechanism for appeal is not clearly laid down, the process can cause a good deal of resentment. This is not the place to speculate about how the procedure could be improved (although I am sure it could), but we should bear in mind that *any* procedure which confers status on some and not on others will cause some resentment occasionally – especially when those conferring the status are themselves making what appears to be a subjective judgment.

Entries at championship shows have, until recently, climbed steadily for many years. There does now appear to be a levelling out but, as yet, no sign of a sustained fall. If the sales of books about dogs and the weekly canine press are anything to go by, interest in the world of show dogs continues to grow.

2 The Exhibitor

Dog shows are for the exhibitor. It is dog owners who generate the demand for dog shows and it is a demand that arises for all sorts of reasons. The primary reason is that success at a show gives the exhibitor and breeder a measure of their success in terms of the quality of the dog. A single success is not enough, of course: some judges are better than others and the quality of the dogs entered at one particular show may not be very high. A win under these circumstances is obviously less valuable.

A serious exhibitor is really out to prove, beyond all doubt, that his or her dog is the best. There will always be disagreements as to which dog is, ultimately, the best, but a consistent series of wins is the most reliable, and indeed the only, guide for both breeder and exhibitor. However good the dog is that you have got at home it is of no value in the show ring unless it wins consistently. (It may be an ideal brood bitch or stud dog, of course, for there are all sorts of perfectly acceptable reasons why a dog is not or cannot be shown.)

In the long term, the breeder of winning dogs (often the exhibitor but not always) measures success by winning regularly with generation after generation of their stock. Dog shows provide the opportunity to test the results of breeding programmes so that the best quality pedigree dogs can be bred, and to provide the records necessary for further improvement in future generations. For those of us deeply involved in the world of show dogs, there is little to match the sight of a quality dog, of whatever breed, moving smoothly around the ring. Such a dog is often a companion and friend to the owner, with all the pleasure that the 'man and his dog' relationship implies, but the exhibitor is looking for something more than this. There is pleasure, pride and status in owning a superb example of a dog just as there is in owning anything of grace and beauty which has artistic merit and receives critical acclaim.

These ideas may sound highfalutin, but I believe that they are the fundamental reasons behind the importance and success of dog shows. There are others, of course, but however important these are to individual exhibitors, the future quality of pedigree dogs must remain paramount.

Despite rapidly increasing costs, a dog show remains a relatively cheap day out. Exhibitors have the opportunity to meet their friends, discuss the latest gossip and, perhaps, have the thrill of a win, all for a few pounds and a car journey. If you start to add up the total costs of even a successful exhibitor making up a Champion, the bottom line sounds horrendous. The majority of exhibitors can travel hopefully but most recognize that this level must, necessarily, be beyond that which their dogs can achieve. They are content to travel to their local shows, plus a few of their favourite championship shows for the occasional prize. The expenses of this level of exhibition are a good deal lower than those of most hobbies, whether they be going to the theatre, fishing, or model railways.

Whatever the competition and whatever the prize, you always take the best dog home

Despite all this, the 'average' exhibitor shows dogs for a relatively short period of time. Precise figures are difficult to obtain, but in a survey of catalogues of the largest championship shows it seems that the average 'life' of an exhibitor is about three years. Put another way, it you look at the catalogue of any championship show and compare it with a catalogue of the same show of five years previously, only 20 per cent of the exhibitors will still be showing. However, of that 20 per cent, it is likely that as many as 80 per cent will still be showing in a further five years. What this boils down to is that the vast majority of exhibitors show for a relatively short time, but that if they survive the first four or five years, they are likely to become established members of the world of show dogs.

Now I do not know how this compares with other leisure activities, but I suspect dogs has a rather higher turnover than most. I also suspect that there is one major reason for this, although, naturally, there are many subsidiary ones.

Of the many hundreds of dogs entered at shows every week of the year, only a small proportion can win a prize. Despite the fact that judges are not always competent, the best dogs usually win. And they tend to belong to established breeders and exhibitors simply because they have a clearer idea of what the 'best' dog looks like. This is not to say that the newcomer does not stand a chance. There are dozens of examples of exhibitors who have made up a Champion with their very first dog (I am one of them) but, in general, new exhibitors think that they will 'have a go' at showing their dog after they have bought it, and nine times out of ten the breeder never expected the dog to be shown and it is just not good enough to win.

Sometimes it does win and this provides an incentive, but most exhibitors who seldom or never win, quite naturally, drop out of showing. A few get bitten by the showing bug, recognize that their dog is not a 'winner' and purchase another of better quality. Alternatively, if they have a bitch they mate her and hope that one of their puppies is better than the dam but, either way, the number of exhibitors who survive initial failure is very few. Added to this, showing is a time- and money-consuming business and so, even if reasonably successful, many potential exhibitors are lost in the early stages for all sorts of financial and personal reasons.

In fact, I believe some of these would stay the course were they made more welcome by their breed club(s). The present situation is much better than it was a few years ago as more people involved are conscious of the importance of public relations, but I do have the feeling that, although newcomers are welcomed by their local training club and general canine society (if they hold regular meetings), the breed clubs do not always make the effort. They often take the attitude that new exhibitors should be thrown in the deep end, learn to swim or get out of the pool. I shall have more to say about this in a future section, but it is an attitude which new exhibitors should be aware exists in some breeds and should be regarded as just another hurdle. The exhibitors who are going to be members of that established 15–20 per cent have to be determined and tough – as well as talented.

The First Stage

The serious exhibitor begins by buying the best show dog he or she can afford. As already explained, most people just buy a dog of a particular pedigree and only afterwards think about showing. They will have decided to get a dog or a bitch, depending on their own preference or experience and the advice they have received from friends or their breeder.

Exhibitors do not always have the facilities or the inclination to breed dogs and, therefore, whether they have a dog or a bitch may appear to matter little. But, whether you are successful or unsuccessful, the time will come when you wish to have another dog to show and this can lead to complications. (The 'life' of a show dog can be many years if it is a good one and can continue to win, but you will certainly want to bring out a youngster after a couple of years, however good the first dog. If the first dog is not successful in the show ring, there is little pleasure in campaigning it, so you would want another dog anyway.)

My advice to the serious exhibitor, whether or not they intend to breed, is: 'Buy the very best bitch you can afford.' Apart from the fact that if she is good but does not win she may still be a good brood bitch (there are lots of reasons why good dogs do not win in the show ring) you, at least, always have the opportunity of having one litter and retaining and showing a dog you have bred yourself – always a more satisfying experience. It is true that it is more difficult to take top honours with a bitch than a dog, but I believe that in the long run it is entirely worth it. You are much less likely to see puppies sired by your dog in the ring than puppies you have bred and kept to show. A dog that wins well does, of course, stand the chance of being used at stud but, in general, breeders with bitches they want to mate want to use a dog (and an owner) with a 'track record' that they can evaluate from pedigree and stud book. This is not to say that many successful exhibitors and breeders have not started their career with a dog. I just believe that it makes for more complications – and you can do without those when you begin showing.

It is all very well for me to tell you to buy the best you can afford, but it is not advice that is always easy to follow. Firstly, you must be prepared to be patient. It may easily take a year or more to find what you are looking for, so, even though you may just strike lucky, it is not worth trying to force the pace.

I believe that you should begin by going to a number of the championship shows at which the breed you like is scheduled. Details can be obtained from the canine press and your breed club. Armed with a catalogue over several shows (this is most important as you need to see the results of several different judges) mark the placings so that you can refer to them later and underline those winning dogs that you personally like. Talk to exhibitors and breeders, too, but try not to take too much notice of what they say. Most exhibitors, quite rightly, believe their own dogs to be the best and will, deliberately or unconsciously, try to influence you. The important aspect of this exercise is to go to as many championship shows or breed open shows as you can. The greater your information, the more likely you will get what you want.

This is what you are looking for: a breeder whose stock wins consistently and whose stock, or descendants, win consistently when owned and handled by other people. This last is a vital requirement. There are plenty of breeders who exhibit their own stock and win very well, but are reluctant to sell quality puppies to others – particularly to a potentially serious exhibitor! The people to talk to are those who own and win with stock bred by that breeder and their advice and assessment can often be of great value. They will, naturally, think that their breeder is the best, but they will tend to be more objective and can tell you whether they got a good winning dog by accident or whether a request for a good puppy was fulfilled.

No wonder it is difficult to choose the best puppy! Some experienced breeders and exhibitors seem to be able to do it after only a few minutes' examination. Others get it wrong if they have lived with the pups for eight weeks!

You may now have narrowed down your choice of breeder and at this stage you need to look at the dogs you underlined as the ones you personally liked. Every kennel will breed a slightly different dog. They will put the emphasis in their breeding on different aspects of the breed and this will necessarily lead to their producing a slightly different 'type'.

As a discerning owner, you will want a dog that you can appreciate and admire, as well as win with, so this must be taken into consideration when you make your choice.

The next thing to do is to meet the breeder formally to discuss the purchase of a puppy. Remember there is no way that the breeder can guarantee to supply you with a top-quality dog that will win. They can try and, if they have undertaken to try, they are legally bound to carry out that request to the best of their ability, but the results cannot be guaranteed. If you want to be absolutely sure of the best, you must buy a mature adult with a good record of wins as well as a good pedigree, but this is likely to be much more expensive.

A good breeder may suggest a puppy from a particular mating, ie one that has proved successful in the past, but, as with everything, you will have to pay for the service you receive and you might find this, too, prohibitive.

By this stage, I would be inclined to 'take a chance'. If the breeder knows that you are a serious exhibitor and that you intend to show the dog, it would be foolish to sell you a puppy of poor quality if your intention and request for a good dog have been made known. You should also, by this time, have established your own and the breeder's credentials, so you should have a good idea of whether you can trust them.

Even after all this and however good your dog is, do not expect to walk into the ring and begin carrying off first prizes. You may do so, of course, but you will be competing against other very good dogs handled by exhibitors of long experience who can make the very best of the dog they are showing. It may take some time, even years, to achieve their standards of handling and showmanship.

Before Entering a Show

Between the time you get your puppy and its first show, apart from the normal training and vaccination, you have to constantly remember that it is going to be a show dog. The first puppy gets all the experience and handling it needs, simply because they are shown off to friends, taken everywhere and generally made to feel important. This is not always true of subsequent puppies, because as soon as there is more than one dog in the household, one will inevitably dominate the other and the underdog (literally in this case) will not get the special and individual treatment of the first. Certainly, as the canine family grows, it becomes increasingly difficult to give the youngsters the sort of experience they need if their potential is to be realized. It is important to bear in mind the way in which your first dog was treated and handled and to ensure that each new puppy bought or retained from a litter does get the wealth and breadth of experience for it to be able to go into the show ring without thinking that all hell has broken loose.

One vital point for both novice and experienced exhibitors is often not thoroughly practised. This is ensuring that the dog will allow his teeth to be looked at without fuss. It is important that a show dog is used to being handled by strangers as well as being used to other unaccustomed happenings and noises. It is a good idea for puppies (as soon as they are old enough) to be taken along to training classes regularly, especially if they do not get out and about otherwise.

Training classes also help the novice exhibitor to understand what is expected of a handler in the ring. Because it looks so simple when viewed from the ringside, many exhibitors assume that handling is easy. When I started showing, my handling was the subject of much good-natured ridicule and even by the time I handled a bitch I had bred to her first Challenge Certificate, the judge commented in the report that 'both dog and handler could do with more ring training'.

The exhibitor must remember that the judge only has a very short time to assess the dog and, if he has to struggle to see the dog's teeth, cannot see the dog move, cannot look at it standing because it is jumping about and turning round, he is entitled to miss it out, however good it might be. Most judges want to see a dog's expression at its best, examine its mouth, 'go over it' to assess its construction – something that is not always easy when it has a profuse or thick coat – and see it stand and move. All this in the space of about ninety seconds. Handling is the art of enabling the judge to do this and presenting the dog in a way that emphasizes its good points and minimizes any poor ones.

Preparation and Presentation for Exhibition

Emphasizing the good points and minimizing the poor ones takes us naturally into the preparation of dogs for exhibition. The amount of preparation depends greatly on the breed, but there are things that are common to all.

It should not be necessary to emphasize cleanliness, but far too many dogs are shown which are actually dirty. Many breeds seldom need bathing, but they should be brushed or polished (that is not a joke – a damp chamois leather can do wonders!) so that they are a pleasure to show and a pleasure to judge. Presenting a mucky dog shows a lack of concern for the dog and little respect for the judge!

Apart from this, all dogs, be they show or pet, should have clean teeth, clipped nails and clean ears and it should go without saying that they should be presented in the show ring in the best possible condition.

There is a bit more to the term 'condition' than meets the eye. What is good condition for a Saluki or an Afghan would be considered emaciated by a breeder of Labradors. Dogs of different breeds are expected to carry varying amounts of muscle and fat. Personally, I believe you do not do your dog any favours by allowing it to carry surplus fat, but there is a tendency among some exhibitors of breeds which are supposed to be well-covered with muscle and give the appearance of stability and solidity to allow them to carry far too much weight. There is also a tendency for exhibitors of large breeds to give too much food in the early months of growth to try to ensure that they 'make size'. Research indicates that such actions can actually be damaging to the dog in the long term. Genetically, the heritability of height in the dog is 90–95 per cent. The increase in height that can be forced by feeding is actually very small and is a pointless exercise. This is not true of bulk and weight, of course, but it is just as unhealthy for dogs to be over- or underweight as it is for us.

Condition is a term also used about the general health of a dog. Judges are not entitled to diagnose whether or not a dog is actually ill, but they will expect clear eyes and nose, the skin to be free of any infection or parasites and for the dog to have a general air of wellbeing. Conditioning is the sum of feeding, exercise and care. It does not rely on expensive supplements, oils or additives. A correct, preferably professionally designed and manufactured, diet ensures that your dog has all the correct nutrients required so, unless you are feeding a home-produced mixed diet, no additives are required.

That being said, some breeds do require special treatment, as their digestive systems are subject to special stresses. There is a number of excellent books on the subject of feeding but your breeder or breed publications are often the best guide.

On the subject of advice from experts and breed publications, there are many breeds that require highly specialized preparation before they can be taken into the ring. In some cases this only consists of bathing and brushing, but in others tradition or fashion decree that a great deal of careful stripping, grooming and clipping is necessary. In some breeds the coat is tied back with small bows or bands to achieve certain effects and in others the coat is sculpted to alter or 'improve' the shape of the head or the conformation of the dog. No general book can tell you how to do this. Publications by the specialist press and the breed clubs are very helpful but, even then, the presentation of such breeds is so highly specialized that only by discussion and demonstration by experts, plus a great deal of practice, does anyone learn the techniques which are virtually an art form.

Many people sincerely believe that the art of presentation and handling is sometimes – even often – used to win with an inferior dog, but I believe that this is usually just sour grapes. The skills we are discussing can only be perfected over many years and there is no point in using them on inferior material.

If a sculptor finds a flaw in his material, he starts again and we have to recognize that those who have the greatest experience and talent in presenting and showing dogs are likely to be those who can select the best before they begin work. As always, long term success is the key to the quality of the dog and, if many experts agree, then you can be sure the dog is of good quality. This does not mean that it is perfect, just that the major virtues outweigh what are, generally, minor faults.

Underneath all this coat is a West Highland White Terrier. It does not look much like a good example of the breed at present, but it will, given a little time and effort

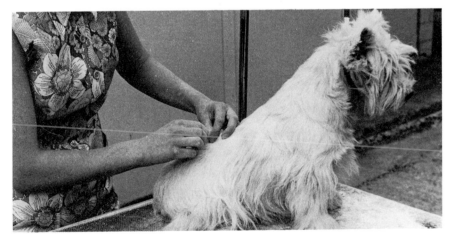

Making the most of a Terrier coat is a skilled business – and very hard work. Stripping out takes time and considerable patience

How about that? Two hours later and ready to go into the show ring

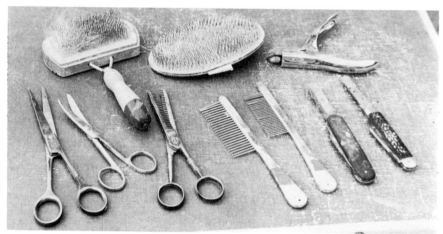

The Terrier enthusiast's toolkit

Paperwork

I hate paperwork, and other dog people being usually of a happy, practical nature usually hate it too. But it has to be done, so it is sensible to get into a routine and stick to it.

The first requirement is that the dog you intend to show must, if it is to be entered in your name, be registered at the Kennel Club by the breeder and then transferred to you. There are innumerable stories about the difficulties of carrying out this simple operation (some of them quite unrepeatable), but it is usually a straightforward process. After the breeder has registered the puppy, you will be sent a transfer form. A breeder who is good at paperwork might even give it to you when you buy your puppy but, I am afraid that if you bought one of mine you would have to wait a few weeks!

When you get the form, half of which should be completed by the breeder, you complete it and send it, with the fee, to the Kennel Club. The Kennel Club will then send you a card and a notification of when the announcement will appear in the supplement to the *Kennel Gazette*. Keep the card in your file that you should have for every dog. In it should be its pedigree, Kennel Club registration card, vaccination certificates and its show records. Incidentally, if you bought the dog you should also insist on and safely keep a receipt. This is the 'legal' proof that the dog really belongs to you. In cases of dispute (fortunately rare), the Kennel Club papers are not considered evidence of owner-ship.

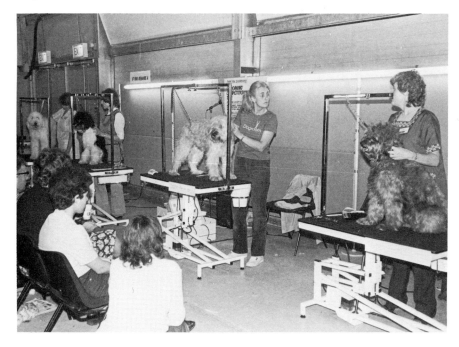

The art of trimming takes a long time to learn properly. Here, finalists in the UK National Grooming Championships are just beginning work on their final test

You are now ready to enter a show. As I have already indicated, you would be sensible to belong to at least one breed club and a local canine society, preferably one which runs training classes as well as shows. Here you will find out which shows are going to be held locally and when they are. Most serious exhibitors also take one of the weekly dog papers, *Our Dogs* or *Dog World*. They carry advertisements from the various canine societies which, apart from the date and venue of the show, list the breeds being scheduled. Few shows (even the very biggest) schedule every breed. Most shows schedule the more popular ones, so if you have an Afghan, Miniature Poodle or Golden Retriever, you will have a choice of show every week, if you so wish. If you have a Tibetan Spaniel, Flat-Coated Retriever or an Elkhound, there will be far fewer classes available and you may have to travel rather further to compete. Almost all shows also schedule 'not separately classified classes', too, and if your breed is not scheduled you can enter in these. You can also enter 'variety' classes and here you will be competing against breeds which were entered in breed classes at the show.

Write to or telephone the secretary of the show for a schedule. This lists all the rules of the show, the entry fees, the classes available and the judge. It also comes with an entry form and it is this you must complete to enter the show. Entry forms are quite straightforward, but it is essential that they are completed carefully and accurately in block capital letters. Even if you only spell the name of the sire or dam of your dog incorrectly your dog could be disqualified from any prize won, so it really is important to you.

Firstly, you need to put in the correct kennel name of the dog. If the full registration papers have not been received from the Kennel Club you need to put NAF (which means Name Applied For) after the name and you should put TAF (Transfer Applied For) if the formalities of transfer of the dog to your ownership have not been completed at the Kennel Club.

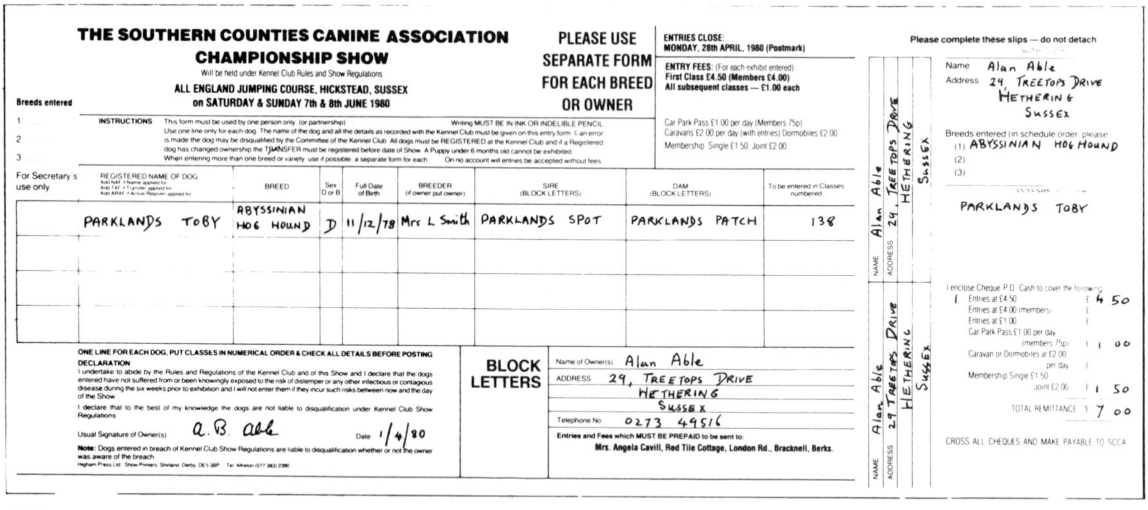

THE SOUTHERN COUNTIES CANINE ASSOCIATION
CHAMPIONSHIP SHOW
Will be held under Kennel Club Rules and Show Regulations
ALL ENGLAND JUMPING COURSE, HICKSTEAD, SUSSEX
on SATURDAY & SUNDAY 7th & 8th JUNE 1980

PLEASE USE SEPARATE FORM FOR EACH BREED OR OWNER

ENTRIES CLOSE: MONDAY, 28th APRIL, 1980 (Postmark)

ENTRY FEES: (For each exhibit entered)
First Class £4.50 (Members £4.00)
All subsequent classes — £1.00 each

Car Park Pass £1.00 per day (Members 75p)
Caravans £2.00 per day (with entries) Dormobiles £2.00
Membership Single £1.50. Joint £2.00

Breeds entered
1
2
3

INSTRUCTIONS This form must be used by one person only (or partnership). Writing MUST BE IN INK OR INDELIBLE PENCIL. Use one line only for each dog. The name of the dog and all the details as recorded with the Kennel Club must be given on this entry form. If an error is made the dog may be disqualified by the Committee of the Kennel Club. All dogs must be REGISTERED at the Kennel Club and if a Registered dog has changed ownership the TRANSFER must be registered before date of Show. A Puppy under 6 months old cannot be exhibited. When entering more than one breed or variety, use if possible, a separate form for each. On no account will entries be accepted without fees.

For Secretary's use only	REGISTERED NAME OF DOG (Add NAF if Name applied for; Add TAF if Transfer applied for; Add ARAF if Active Register applied for)	BREED	Sex D or B	Full Date of Birth	BREEDER (if owner put owner)	SIRE (BLOCK LETTERS)	DAM (BLOCK LETTERS)	To be entered in Classes numbered
	PARKLANDS TOBY	ABYSSINIAN HOG HOUND	D	11/12/78	Mrs L Smith	PARKLANDS SPOT	PARKLANDS PATCH	138

ONE LINE FOR EACH DOG, PUT CLASSES IN NUMERICAL ORDER & CHECK ALL DETAILS BEFORE POSTING

DECLARATION
I undertake to abide by the Rules and Regulations of the Kennel Club and of this Show and I declare that the dogs entered have not suffered from or been knowingly exposed to the risk of distemper or any other infectious or contagious disease during the six weeks prior to exhibition and I will not enter them if they incur such risks between now and the day of the Show.

I declare that to the best of my knowledge the dogs are not liable to disqualification under Kennel Club Show Regulations.

Usual Signature of Owner(s) A. B. Able Date 1/4/80

Note: Dogs entered in breach of Kennel Club Show Regulations are liable to disqualification whether or not the owner was aware of the breach.

Higham Press Ltd. Show Printers. Shirland. Derby. DE5 3BP. Tel. Alfreton (077 383) 2390

BLOCK LETTERS

Name of Owner(s) Alan Able
ADDRESS 29, TREETOPS DRIVE
HETHERING
SUSSEX
Telephone No 0273 49516

Entries and Fees which MUST BE PREPAID to be sent to:
Mrs. Angela Cavill, Red Tile Cottage, London Rd., Bracknell, Berks.

NAME Alan Able
ADDRESS 24, TREETOPS DRIVE
HETHERING
SUSSEX

NAME Alan Able
ADDRESS 29 TREETOPS DRIVE
HETHERING
SUSSEX

Please complete these slips — do not detach

Name Alan Able
Address 24, TREETOPS DRIVE
HETHERING
SUSSEX

Breeds entered (in schedule order please)
(1) ABYSSINIAN HOG HOUND
(2)
(3)

PARKLANDS TOBY

I enclose Cheque P.O. Cash to cover the following

1 Entries at £4.50	£	4 50
Entries at £4.00 (members)	£	
Entries at £1.00	£	
Car Park Pass £1.00 per day (members 75p)	£	1 00
Caravan or Dormobiles at £2.00 per day	£	
Membership Single £1.50 Joint £2.00	£	1 50
TOTAL REMITTANCE	£	7 00

CROSS ALL CHEQUES AND MAKE PAYABLE TO SCCA

FIG. 4

This is followed by the date of birth and then by the name of the breeder (you put Br. Ex. for Exhibitor, if you bred the dog yourself). This is followed by the full kennel name of the sire and then the full kennel name of the dam. If you are entering for Crufts, you also have to put the show at which the dog 'qualified' to enter and these 'qualifying classes', which are only available where the breed has been allocated Challenge Certificates, are announced each year in the *Kennel Gazette* and reprinted in the canine press.

At the end of the line is a space for the classes in which you want the dog. Which class you enter will depend on the age and the amount of winning your dog has done. A full list of the 'Definitions of Classes' is not included here because they change occasionally and are, in any case, set out in every schedule. However, to give you an idea what is involved, if your dog is less than nine months old on the first day of the show it can be entered in the Minor Puppy Class. You are not restricted to this (or any other class, so long as you fulfil the requirements of the class in other respects), but it is sensible to put a youngster into Minor Puppy rather than Open where it will be, possibly, competing with Champions. Dogs less than twelve months are classified as puppies and those less than eighteen months as juniors. Apart from these classes, entry is restricted by the number of wins (at that level) the dog has had. If your dog is successful you will quickly find it cannot be entered in the Novice or Maiden classes and the very successful dogs quickly go out of Graduate and Post Graduate classes, too. Study the definition of classes carefully, and study the entries at the shows in your breed so that you can estimate the best level at which to enter your dog.

Incidentally, each first prize in breed classes at an open show counts as one point and each first prize at a Championship Show at which Challenge Certificates are on offer is worth three points. If your dog can collect 25 points before the age of eighteen months, then it is entitled to a Junior Warrant Certificate. You have to apply to the Kennel Club for this - but it is free.

The entry form usually includes a space for you to work out how much the whole exercise is costing you and you must send your cheque or a postal order with your entry. You are also required to sign a statement saying that you will not take your dog if it comes into contact with any infectious disease prior to the show. This is extremely important. Your dog may be vaccinated up to the occiput but, whatever the temptation, please do not take the dog if it has come into contact with any infection. Please, too, fill out separate entry forms for each dog if they are of different breeds if breed classes are scheduled. If you do not, the secretary has to copy them out before they can be sent to the printer and it is a very time-consuming job. You do not have to use the official entry form for the show (just cross through the name of the canine society at the top and replace it with the show you are entering). Anything will do - even a sheet of paper - so long as the 'infectious' clause is signed on one of the forms.

The schedule and entry form will also include the date on which entries close. Secretaries like exhibitors who send their entry forms in plenty of time – but most people do not! You must have the letter in the post box before the last collection on the day of closing of entries. The date on the envelope usually dictates whether or not your entry will be accepted. Many, varied and wonderful are the stories told by secretaries about exhibitors who have forgotten to post their entries. The best excuse I ever heard was when a prospective exhibitor at Southern Counties telephoned two weeks after the closing date to ask whether he could enter at the show 'under the circumstances'. The 'circumstances' were that his wife had given the entry form and cheque to post to his mother, who had, unfortunately, had a heart attack and died while out that afternoon. He had only just received the 'effects' back and among them was his wife's entry. She had died on the way *to* the post box, not on the way back.

One problem secretaries have is what to do about entries which arrive several days after the closing of entries, but stamped by a franking machine. The exhibitor is late but does not think it matters because they can post the entry in their firm's post and alter the date to that previous to closing of entries. Once in the Post Office system, it never gets discovered and can turn up two weeks later looking as if it was just delayed in the post. We get several of these every year, although some exhibitors, in their hurry, get confused and date their cheque or entry form with the actual date and not the postage date! The first time this happened, a friend of mine remarked that the entry was 'perfectly franked, but dishonest'.

Having posted your entries in plenty of time, you now have to sit back and wait. The bigger societies usually send you an exhibitors pass to get into the show and, if you can prepay car parking or for your catalogue, you will usually get a voucher to cover these. Most smaller shows have now dispensed with this to save some money (and work, of course) and the exhibitors just turn up at the show.

You may arrive to find that your name is not included in the catalogue because the secretary has not received your entry. This seldom happens, but if it does the show must allow you to show your dog and it is then your responsibility to prove to the Kennel Club that you actually posted the entry. More paperwork, I am afraid, but to ensure peace of mind and save a great deal of work you should get a 'Proof of Posting' certificate when your entry is sent. This is issued free on request by the Post Office and is a very good idea. It does mean passing your letter over a Post Office counter rather than slipping it into a letter box, but the extra trouble is well worth it.

Just before the show you should give some thought to what you will need and what you will wear. The latter may seem silly, but you have to take into account whether or not judging will be out-of-doors, the time of year, and your own comforts. It is not sensible to wear high heels, coats that flap (and cover up your ring number), anything that dangles and is likely to get in the way, or clothes that are easily damaged. In some breeds the handler's ensemble is almost part of the dog's performance but, for most of us, sensible and comfortable clothes are best, which do not distract the dogs or the judge.

In your show bag you need:

Ring clip – for holding your ring number.
Grooming equipment – if required.
Water – in a glass bottle to prevent unattractive 'taste'. (Always use water from the dog's usual supply.)

If the show is benched, you will also need:

Benching chain – to attach to the dog's collar and to the ring of the bench.
Blanket – not really necessary, but aesthetically more pleasing than the bare boards of the bench.

Many exhibitors take their chairs, picnic tables and full lunch and, if you are having a proper day out, this can make a bit more of it, but it can be a lot to lug about! I always travel with waterproofs and wellingtons, too, working on the principle that it is 'less likely to rain if I am properly prepared for the worst'.

At the Show

The best single piece of advice for any exhibitor is to arrive at the show in plenty of time. There is nothing worse than sitting in the car wondering if you will make your class. Your tension will certainly be picked up by your dog and all that hard work and training will go out of the window. You must have time on arrival at the show to exercise and play with your dog. It must be an exciting and enjoyable occasion which he will look forward to in the future. The worse thing you can do, however experienced you and your dog are, is to rush into the ring at the last moment, not having had time to look up your ring number, change to your show lead or attend the calls of nature.

When you arrive at the show find your bench, if the show is benched, settle your dog and relax. Most exhibitors buy a catalogue which becomes an important part of their records for the future if they are serious exhibitors or breeders. There are several ways in which catalogues can be laid out but, however it is done, it will tell you which dog you have entered in which class and what other dogs are entered. Better catalogues include an index, the number and location of the ring in which you are to be judged and the time at which judging should start. Depending on the show management these details are helpful guides or frustrating fiction. You will soon learn which shows provide the sort of service that you, as an exhibitor, approve and the ones which you would prefer to avoid.

When your class is called, you take your dog into the ring. The steward will give you your ring number and tell you where to stand. Some benched shows leave the ring numbers on the benches so, if you find a spare one (the other is above the bench) then it has not been dropped by accident – you will need it in the ring!

Most large shows are benched. Each dog has its own bench and, in theory, only one dog is allowed on a bench. But exhibitors do not ⁀lways follow this rule, a shown by these two benched Afghans

IN THE RING

As you enter the ring and throughout the class you must keep two things at the forefront of your mind. (Unfortunately, they are mutually exclusive and this is one of the reasons why showing dogs is more difficult than it looks.) The first is that you must concentrate on your dog all the time to make sure that it is always looking its best. Even in a big class where all the exhibitors are relaxed and the dogs are not showing, you should still keep a sharp eye on your dog. You can talk to other exhibitors or to someone outside the ring, but the pose of the dog in front of you, whether standing, sitting or lying down should still be attractive. A dog that is taking an intelligent interest in what is going on is more likely to catch the judge's eye than one which curls up and goes to sleep.

These two pictures show clearly the importance of the handler when it comes to presenting a dog. This Champion Greyhound looks more than respectable in the first picture but in the second it looks dull and listless because its neck is not gracefully arched

The second skill you must acquire is to follow the judge's directions exactly. The judge will expect you to have watched the other exhibits being judged and by the time you reach him you should have taken in his routine. Your dog is likely to be given less consideration if the judge is expecting you to move the dog in a triangle and you take off straight up and down!

The problem is that many exhibitors concentrate so fully on their dog that they virtually ignore the judge, or they are so anxious to get it right that they trip over their lead. What a judge generally wants is to be able to look at the dog standing (on the table if it is one of the small breeds) for a few seconds, so that he can take in the general picture. He may well want to walk around the dog to assess front and rear stance too, so your dog must stand still. Of course, it should still give the appearance of being alert – no one wins with a stodgy pudding, however good it is otherwise.

The judge will then approach the dog, usually from the front, and will want to examine its mouth, feel its skeletal structure, musculature and quality of coat along with the other features which cannot be assessed from a distance. He will then want to see the dog move and will ask you to take the dog straight up and down the ring, or ask you to take it to a corner across in front of him, to another corner and then back towards him. If the judge wants you to do this he will say, 'Triangle, please'. He expects you to move your dog at the trot and it is important that you have practised this, preferably under the eyes of someone knowledgeable. Every dog has its best speed and you need to know this, as going faster or more slowly will not allow the dog to be seen at its best.

On your return to the judge, stop several feet in front of him. No one wants to be run over by a dog in the ring. This is a very common fault by exhibitors, so stop well short of the judge and stand the dog so he has a further chance to examine it. Some breeds are 'gaited' rather differently to others. German Shepherd Dogs, for instance, are expected to move at the flying trot around the ring with the judge in the centre and many judges do this, in any case, at the beginning of a class to help the dogs to settle and to give them a preliminary look.

Once your dog has been seen, you return to the end of the line. Different judges organize their rings in different ways, so you need to follow the steward's or the judge's directions and make sure before you go into the class that you know what the ring procedure is.

When the judge has seen all the dogs, he will probably look over all of them from a distance yet again. At this stage, if there are any dogs in the ring which he has already seen from a previous class, he will look at these too.

Finally, you should set up your dog in line with the other exhibitors

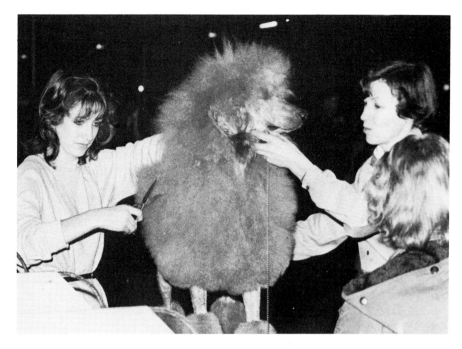

Getting a dog ready for the show ring can take hours. Here a Poodle is being given its final trim

for the judge to choose the winners. You may be asked to move your dog again but, eventually, the judge will select a number of dogs that he wishes to remain in the ring, either for him to place or for further assessment. Some judges pick out ten or more dogs for further assessment from a big class, others will bring out their first prize winner, then their second and so on, placing them as they pick them out. With a good dog, plus skill and luck, you will be placed or even win a class. It's a great thrill and if you can win occasionally you will enjoy showing. Do not worry if you do not win – even if you and your friends think you should have. If you show regularly there will be times that you win when you should not have done and this will make up for it! There are plenty of poor judges and good judges sometimes make mistakes. Be patient. If you have a good dog and you show it at the right level, you ought to pick up a prize card occasionally, even in the well-supported breeds.

If you win your class or in a mixed class you have only been beaten by dogs of the opposite sex, you can challenge for best of sex. At the end of the judging of each sex, or of the breed if there are mixed classes, the judge selects the best of sex from those dogs which are unbeaten. These dogs come into the ring as if it was a normal class although, of course, the judge does not have to go over each dog again. He may wish to move the dogs again to refresh his memory or make more careful comparisons, but he will usually soon choose which he likes best. At bigger shows the judge will also be asked to allocate a Reserve Best of Sex and this is certainly expected at a championship show.

Finally, the two dogs judged to be Best of Sex meet for the judge to decide which is Best of Breed. Should you reach these heights you are then entitled to go into the group ring, where your dog is judged once again – the full procedure this time, as it is often another judge who awards Best in Group. Then, finally, the six best group winners compete for Best in Show – often another judge again. At some smaller shows the 'group' stage is omitted, but this does not alter the basic procedure. At a championship show each Best of Sex receives a Challenge Certificate, if they are on offer, and each Reserve to the CC winner gets a Reserve Challenge Certificate.

VARIETY CLASSES

This has all assumed that you have been entered in breed classes, ie those that are scheduled for one breed only. However, there are two sorts of variety classes that you should know about. (There are, in fact, special variety classes occasionally allowed by the Kennel Club, such as the Pedigree Chum Special Stakes Classes, but these are exceptional.) If your breed is not scheduled at a show, you may enter your dog in Not Separately Classified Classes. In these classes you will meet a number of dogs of different breeds, none of whom have classes scheduled. A judge of wide experience has been appointed (in theory, at any rate) and the classes are judged in the same way as the breed classes, the eventually Best NSC dog going into the appropriate group ring.

After Best in Show has been judged, many societies put on variety classes. (In fact, for technical reasons some variety puppy classes are put on before Best in Show, but the principle is the same) and any dog entered at the show may be entered in these classes. They are straightforward and there are no subsequent challenges at the end of the show.

ETIQUETTE FOR EXHIBITORS

We have already discussed the importance of clearly and accurately completing entry forms and of getting them in on time, but it will do no harm to mention it again for it is very important.

There is no penalty for not attending a show you have entered, although usually you will forfeit the entry fee. However, if you are entered in more than one class, you must go into both of them, even if you were not placed in the first one, unless you have the judge's specific permission to withdraw. If you arrive late and miss your class, you forfeit your entry fee also. Some exhibitors believe that if they arrive late they can take their dog into the Open class, but this is not the case. You can, with the show manager's and the judge's permission, go into the Open class if, and only if, your dog has been entered in the wrong class on your entry form. (If the mistake is a printer's error in the catalogue, of course, you can go into the class you actually entered, but you must see the show secretary to make sure that it *is* a printer's error and to get an official note for the steward to transfer you.) If you have entered a dog in minor puppy when it should have been in puppy, you may transfer to the puppy class and you may transfer to the appropriate class if you have entered it in the wrong breed, the wrong sex or the wrong colour!

During a show you may come under pressure from other exhibitors. There is a certain and continuing element of gamesmanship in the ring, which you will learn fast enough if you keep your wits about you. Such activities are neither polite nor within the spirit of fair competition, but it would be foolish to deny their existence. Experience is the best teacher. It is seldom a problem if you are unsuccessful!

Personally, I think manners maketh the dog show exhibitor just as much as they maketh Man. Those that are going to have the greatest influence on our sport – and that means being involved over many years – have it in their best interests to be both courteous and helpful. It would be a great shame if some of the manners of some professional sportsmen were regularly seen beside or in the show ring. Ultimately, we are all concerned with quality and the welfare of dogs and if this is our first consideration the best should always win and be appreciated for grace and beauty, no matter who it belongs to. This does not mean that there should be no competitive element. When I am in the ring, I am determined to make my dog look its best and win the class. But there is no point in being resentful if you are beaten. You always take the best dogs home.

Finally

This section has been an introduction to the show ring and I have tried to cover all the important points the novice exhibitor needs to know. The next section, although not meant primarily for the exhibitor, nevertheless contains much relevant and helpful information, which I believe exhibitors will find useful and which may also give them a greater insight into the world of show dogs. If you are going to be one of the winning 20 per cent they will repay careful reading.

3 The Show Management

Introduction

Few serious exhibitors show their dogs for very long before they become involved in some part of the organization of the world of dogs. Because of the high turnover of exhibitors, those who stay the course for four or five years almost certainly find that they are at least being asked to help at a show by stewarding, helping in the car park or with refreshments and, if they are willing and enthusiastic, tend to get involved at committee level soon afterwards. Some exhibitors, of course, have special accountancy or secretarial skills and can find themselves in a relatively senior position quite quickly while others will either not be interested or not have the time to be involved.

I often wonder why people allow their time (and their money) to be so completely taken up in organizing activities for other people with virtually no reward. It is just as well that there are so many, for the whole of dog show society would collapse without them just as effectively as if all exhibitors ceased to show.

I believe most people take up their responsibilities because they find that the world of show dogs gives them a great deal of interest and enjoyment and they are pleased to have the opportunity to give something back. A proportion, I am afraid, see an opportunity to profit from being in a position of power, either in terms of judging appointments, becoming known to judges or, financially, through having access to puppy sales or stud fees. Fortunately, there are very few of them but, as in any other field, the trouble that they cause is out of all proportion to their numbers. However, the vast majority seem to take this in their stride and manage to run both clubs and shows despite all manner of problems.

I propose to touch on general society organization in this section, but I shall concentrate on the actual techniques of show management. It must be said that some shows, at all levels, are not well-run and that they are consequently less enjoyable for exhibitors, helpers and judges. There is no need for this and I hope that some of the ideas outlined here will be of assistance.

The scene at an open show. There are not usually as many entries but this does not mean that a keen interest is not taken in the judging

General Canine Society Management

All canine societies, both general and breed, have as their main aim the advancement of dogs in general or a breed in particular. Far too many associations take this as meaning no more than running dog shows, but I believe that every association should take a wider view. Many general canine societies run weekly meetings which encourage newcomers and give them ring experience. They arrange charity events for various canine causes and seminars and instruction for their members. Many breed clubs publish leaflets about their breed and analyses of their standards as well as various news-sheets and yearbooks. Some have schemes for training judges and organize meetings so that newcomers to the breed can learn more of the background. These are the societies who are really fulfilling their aim; they usually have an active and enthusiastic membership and there are few complaints about the way they are run. Members of such committees are usually anxious to improve the services of the society and welcome both constructive criticism and positive suggestions. They are likely to encourage active participation and are usually both productive and successful.

As in every field of activity, canine societies range from the very good to the pretty poor, but the majority do a useful and sensible job. Canine societies have a curious relationship with the Kennel Club. For instance, they cannot run dog shows without Kennel Club approval and, if this is granted, they must be prepared to run it in accordance with the rules and regulations laid down. On the other hand, the Kennel Club will take no responsibility for the running of the society. They will be ticked off, or fined if they transgress Kennel Club rules, but the organization is entirely in the hands of the members who are expected to arrange their own affairs. Their attitude is that if you do not like the way the society is run, then the society's rules (which they have approved) allow you to take the matter into your own hands via the arrangements for calling a special general meeting and, if you have enough support, then you can make the changes required.

Overall, the policy seems to work and with over 1500 canine societies (plus the Kennel Club's policy to allow at least two societies for each breed if there is a demand for it) they argue that everybody has a choice.

Club Structure and Procedures

In a book about showing dogs, a detailed analysis of canine association structure and procedure is not necessary, but I should like to include some of the important aspects of committee work in the ideal situation.

THE COMMITTEE

The committee are the representatives of the members. They take decisions on their behalf and, apart from sharing the work of the society between them, have a duty to try to involve members when and where they can help. Their responsibilities include the selection of judges, the production of a judging list (if a breed society), the general organization of shows and, in a more general sense, guiding and modifying the work of the society.

The committee's responsibilities in relation to the demands made by the Kennel Club are quite specific and should be clearly understood. The most important of these is that the committee promises to 'underwrite' each show and some of their members (which must include chairman, secretary and treasurer) have to take on the responsibility of guarantors and are therefore *personally* responsible for any financial loss incurred and any insurance claim against the society.

These days, even the smallest open show may incur an expenditure of hundreds of pounds and it can be over £75,000 for some of the biggest championship shows. Anyone signing the Kennel Club's Application for a Licensed Show should make sure that the society's funds are sufficient to meet any claim and that the society is adequately insured against Third Party Public Liability claims. In an effort to be competitive and keep down their members' subscriptions, some societies run only on a frayed shoestring and they are just the ones which will also be less well organized and so liable to a greater loss.

The committee are also held responsible for ensuring that the Kennel Club regulations are properly observed. These are extensive and complicated and their interpretation is not always straightforward. Certainly, many members and exhibitors do not fully understand them and committee members often have to be both knowledgeable and tactful. The committee, too, usually have the responsibility of selecting judges for a show, but this aspect of their work is discussed later in the chapter.

THE SECRETARY

The secretary is, in theory, the servant of the committee and carries out their wishes on a day-to-day basis. Some secretaries wield far more power within the societies than this and the committee often delegates quite large areas of responsibility to its secretary. The secretary is responsible for keeping the records of the society (including its minutes and lists of members), communicating with the Kennel Club, its members and the various individuals and organizations that are affected by the society. It is worth mentioning that every decision taken by the society and every appointment or contract made must be clearly written down. Many secretaries rely on the telephone (quite rightly and naturally) but then do not confirm their conversation in writing. It is absolutely essential that this is done. The 'he said', 'she promised' series of statements when things go wrong is totally unsatisfactory unless backed up by letters and replies. Important letters should be sent by recorded delivery and copies of letters and replies must be meticulously filed. The secretary also takes on much of the tasks of running the society's shows and often also the show management as well, although I shall deal with this under another heading.

The secretarial tasks involved in show organization include correspondence with the Kennel Club, preparing the schedule for the printer and arranging its distribution, putting adverts in the canine press and receiving, collating and preparing the catalogue. Some societies appoint a 'show secretary' (and sometimes even a special sub-committee) for these tasks, but they are generally handled by the secretary.

THE CHAIRMAN

However the secretary and treasurer are elected (often directly by the members at the Annual General Meeting), the chairman is usually elected by the committee. This is a most important office because the chairman, by his conduct of committee meetings, can block or hinder innovation and, by the same token, encourage and motivate committee members. Any society (canine or otherwise) is in a weak position if its chairman is not able, efficient, courteous and open-minded. It is a position that all committees should take great care about and we are fortunate in the world of dogs that so many able people are willing to take up these posts.

THE TREASURER

The treasurer of a canine association has the most unenviable job. He has to ensure that the society remains financially viable, has to point out those areas of the society's activities which perhaps need to be curtailed or even dropped, and is the one who has to defend both increases in subscriptions and auditors' quirks in the balance sheet. The job requires a great deal of careful work. A good treasurer is essential to the smooth running of any society.

The officers and committee of most canine societies are given considerable help by relatives and friends who rally round and help with everything from sorting prize cards to selling raffle tickets. We must always remember how much we all rely on the services of so many people who give their time willingly and freely. We would be lost without them for their praises are not always sung as often as they might be. But as a general rule, I do not believe it is in a society's best interests to have close relatives on the same committee, and particularly among the officers. It can and does work in some cases, but it should not be necessary and can cause resentment among members.

Finally, a word of advice to those taking on the responsibilities. I feel I should emphasize how helpful the staff of the Kennel Club can be if any committee member or officer needs advice. Those in charge of the various departments are both knowledgeable and experienced and they are always pleased to help. The Kennel Club has, in fact, published a very useful pamphlet about running a canine society and I would not only highly recommend it, but consider it essential reading for anyone involved.

If the Kennel Club seems distant and faceless, do not be afraid to ask those with more experience than you. When I first took over the Nordic Show, I had virtually no experience of show organization. On the front of the previous schedule the name Ivan Strawson appeared as 'Patron'. I telephoned, explained I did not know what a patron did, said that I had found myself flung into the show circuit pool at the deep end and asked if he could help. Ivan was a very experienced judge, Chief Steward at Southern Counties Championship Show and highly respected. He was the sort of person who, had I been born with less self-confidence, I would not have approached. In the event, he was marvellous. He answered all my questions, travelled 150 miles to get to the show and worked unceasingly throughout the day. He was pleased to help – and no one had ever asked him before! He was a great loss to the world of dogs when he died and it always gives me pleasure to see a copy of the little Foyles Handbook *Showing Dogs* as he is pictured on the front cover.

As a result of that experience, I have never had any hesitation in just asking for help. I have found that it is always forthcoming from those whose primary interest is in the long-term future and development of shows and show dogs.

Successful Show Management and Public Relations

Most canine societies see their main activity in organizing opportunities for their members to show dogs at various levels. The basic show structure has already been discussed in the section of this book devoted to the exhibitor and there is no need to repeat those details. However, the committee of a canine society have a great deal to consider beyond whether their show should be sanction, limited, open or (where appropriate) of championship status and many of these considerations apply to all shows.

The first question that the committee needs to ask itself is: 'What are the needs and demands of our members and our exhibitors?' Many canine societies seldom give such a question much thought. The society's annual 'pattern' is established and they just go on from year to year without making any changes apart from altering the classification slightly. However, the forward-looking canine society will be constantly striving to improve its services and its shows.

It is a good idea to carry out a study once a year and have a meeting at which all the activities of the society are assessed and plans made for two years ahead. This gives time for planning and organization for any changes and enables dates and venues to be booked with confidence. If an assessment is carried out under the headings of: membership (increase or decline); exhibitors (entries at shows); and other activities (training evenings, seminars, publications, etc.), then each succeeding year can be seen as a platform on which to build rather than an end in itself.

As far as shows are concerned, the following questions need to be asked:

Are they being run
    At the right level,
    At the right time,
    In the right place,
    With the right classification?
Are they attracting
    Dogs of quality,
    Exhibitors of experience,
    New exhibitors,
    Regular helpers?

If exhibitors and members constantly complain about the first group and the show secretary is scraping around for entries just before the show, then action needs to be taken. Other signs of an inefficient and unsatisfactory society are the late printing of schedules, little or too late advertising, no one being available or able to answer exhibitors' questions at the show and those doing the work complaining that they never get any help!

Many exhibitors are interested in showing rare breeds. Here is a Japanese Spitz, which has become very popular recently in the UK

If this is the case the whole committee needs to undertake a close examination of their approaches to the problems of running a show. People are pleased to be involved and will help if they can, but they must be motivated (ie they must have a reason to *want* to help), and they must be asked. But ask in plenty of time, in the right way and follow up your conversation with a letter which thanks them and which explains clearly what is involved. Furthermore, be sure that they are thanked for their efforts afterwards. A pre-printed card to stewards, judges, committee and other helpers is all that is required (although if you have the time and energy, personal letters are best) and makes people feel that they are valued and respected for their efforts.

I believe that this positive approach should be used whatever the level of show. A dog does not know the difference between a match and a championship show and the enthusiasm, experience or the desire to learn of any exhibitor must be treated with equal respect.

This does not mean that people must be organized out of existence. There are many who confuse organization and administration with 'telling people what to do'. This attitude necessarily leads to confrontation which, although sometimes inevitable, should be avoided if possible. Those involved in dog shows, at whatever level, do so because they want to – they have a choice of hobby and they could just as well breed and show cats as dogs. They do not want to be pushed from pillar to post on the one hand or left in a vacuum on the other.

I believe the secret is an understanding of both the broad spectrum of the event and attention to detail by the show management. Everybody, from show manager to car park attendant, should know exactly what they are to do and the times when they should be doing it. Exhibitors should be given precise and clear information about every detail of the show so that they, too, know exactly what is happening. My point is best illustrated using an actual example. I am show manager of one of the United Kingdom's major championship shows and I believe it to be well-organized. However, over a number of years, the committee showed concern regarding the presentation of the group and Best in Show competition.

It was difficult to see exactly what was causing the confusion and I am sure that the exhibitors and spectators did not think that there were any problems. But we discovered that, although all the procedures were simple, each person involved in this part of the show knew the aim, but was carrying out his or her responsibilities in a slightly different way. They were also putting emphasis on different aspects of the job. One group steward, for instance, felt that it was very important to get the dogs into the ring in schedule order so a gap occurred between the groups while they were sorted out. Another considered that the dogs should come in as soon as possible after the preceding group so would, without thinking, sacrifice order or completeness of the group, so that there was a lot of shuffling about after the group got into the ring with latecomers trailing in during the judging. My concern was to make sure that everything started exactly on time, so a decision on which group should be first was delayed until we knew which group of breeds was finished so that no one knew until the last moment when they should be ready. There were several other minor inconsistencies, all of which led to a rather untidy, uneven close to the show. I should emphasize that this was not a serious problem and I am sure that few people outside those involved even considered it, but we spent the best part of a committee meeting sorting out our priorities and making decisions of order, allocation of duties and timing, which showed everyone what they and the others should have been doing. The following year everyone knew what was happening and that section of the show ran without a hitch.

I believe that it is vital throughout the whole of the planning of a show that each area of responsibility is discussed, agreed and then put into writing. To be honest, it is almost too easy to mount a dog show and even easier for it to be a shambles! A great deal of time and effort is required, at every level, if it is to have that smooth professionalism which can be achieved and to which exhibitors are entitled.

Appointing Judges

Well before any show (and for the large championship shows this is sometimes four or five years in advance) the committee needs to sit down and select their judges. For a breed society this is usually quite straightforward: the committee will almost certainly know those people eligible and it is just a question of making a choice – although making that choice often takes a good deal of thought and discussion. For the general canine society life is much more difficult. The experience of the committee is likely to be limited largely to their own breeds, but the society will certainly expect to schedule classes for other breeds. The committee will often rely on members of the society making specific recommendations and some societies ask their committee members to make enquiries of those in other breeds and then report back to the committee. Some committees delegate their secretary to arrange judges. This is acceptable occasionally – when a judge drops out close to the show date, for instance – but, in general, this is not good practice and committees should make every effort to avoid it.

Breed clubs circulate their judging lists to the championship shows, and smaller societies, where the number of shows which classify their breed is small, should do the same for open shows. However, this is quite impossible in the bigger breeds although, in these instances, there is often a regional breed society which could and should take on the responsibility for the general canine societies in their area.

Many exhibitors complain that they do not get suitable judges. Frankly, this is often their own fault. Exhibitors should press their own breed clubs and their own societies to take the greatest care in compiling judging lists and appointing judges. The societies themselves, of course, should consult their members and do their best to adhere to their wishes.

Put like this it does sound easy, but judges and appointments are a constant source of controversy. The problems are discussed in a further section, but the solution must be found at committee level because it is they that can, if they have the will, exercise control of lists and appointments.

In the final analysis, the general canine society carries the greatest responsibilities. If they appoint unsuitable judges for breeds, they can allow them to 'clock up' classes so that it becomes very difficult for the Kennel Club to turn them down as experienced enough to give Challenge Certificates – whatever the breed clubs say.

Unfortunately, there is a small proportion of people in the world of show dogs in positions of apparent power who will put on pressure or arrange specific appointments at open and championship show level. Much of this 'negotiation' is done without the knowledge of the committees involved, for who is to say whether a name put forward is really suitable or is someone who has promised the proposer an appointment? There will always be this element, of course. It exists in every area of competition but committees should be aware of it and try to prevent such 'deals' taking place if they possibly can. A society or a group of societies where this happens quickly gets known and shows can lose a great deal in terms of status and entries if it is allowed to continue.

One thing I should like to see every general canine society do is to send out to their members every year (perhaps with the notification of the Annual General Meeting) a questionnaire which requests information about their breed or breeds, their involvement in the breed and their success as breeders and in the show ring. Many exhibitors, quite rightly, do not push themselves forward and many committees, therefore, have no knowledge of the experience or interests of their own members. I should like to see these questionnaires distributed to other canine societies in the area and to provide the basis of future appointments. Local canine societies would be much better able to monitor the standard and progress of judges so appointed for it will quickly become apparent whether or not they receive general approval.

Unfortunately, most committees are so busy that there is no time available for this sort of exercise. However, I do believe that the whole question of appointing judges is one over which general canine societies should take much care. This is particularly true when putting on classes for breeds which are less common and of which the committee has little or no experience. It is always wise in the first instance to approach breed clubs for some indication of the support the classes are likely to enjoy and for a judge who would be acceptable.

Generally, an acceptable all-rounder is likely to command a larger entry than the specialist in the smaller breeds simply because a specialist can be associated with quite a substantial percentage of the possible entry which is therefore unable to compete. As the classes become more established and it is seen to be supported that distinction does tend to become less important.

Once again it must be emphasized that it is essential to ensure that all decisions and invitations are written down, that notes are taken of subsequent action and replies carefully kept and filed.

Secretarial Duties

As already explained, one person often combines the job of secretary, show secretary and show manager, but as these tasks are often delegated it will be more sensible to discuss them separately. Incidentally, my dividing line may not be the same as that of other people, so it is important that secretary and manager sit down and write down where their various responsibilities begin and end!

The secretary's first task in the organization of any show is to apply for permission to hold it from the Kennel Club. Initial application forms are published in the *Kennel Gazette*. This is done quite a long way ahead (at the time of writing – March 1983 – the open show application forms for shows to be held in 1984 have been arriving in the current issue), so a secretary taking over a society may well find that much of this work is completed. The form asks for the dates of your show and if there are any other shows that you particularly do not want to clash with.

The Show Department then collates this information, decides on the dates you will be allowed to hold the show and sends you an official application for a licence to hold the show. This asks for much more information, including the size of the venue, how many dogs the area can accommodate, how much undercover accommodation is available and who the guarantors will be. This last, as explained earlier, is most important as the Kennel Club will take no responsibility for debts incurred by a canine society and the guarantors would be expected to make up the difference from their own pockets if any of the show's invoices could not be paid. Incidentally, before sending this form off to the Kennel Club, you should make a copy of the list of guarantors. You will need it later.

A fee for the licence to run the show is payable at this stage and the amount depends on the size of the show. If all the details are set out properly the Kennel Club then issues the licence which, incidentally, must be displayed on the site during the show.

Once the judges have been selected they must be invited and con-firmed. A standard printed letter with a tear-off reply slip is a good idea if your society puts on a lot of classes. The judge then just has to complete the slip and return it. I find that some judges are often rather late in replying, so a paragraph which says that unless a reply is received within twenty-one days it will be assumed that they are unable to officiate enables you to contact another judge very quickly. As the replies come in they should be ticked off the 'master' list and the names inserted in the appropriate place in the schedule.

At this stage, the secretary needs to prepare the time schedule. A Year Planner of some kind is a great help here, as you can see clearly exactly when things are to be done. The easiest approach is to work backwards from the date of the show, putting in all the dates by which things must be completed. The schedule below is for a championship show taking place on 1 September. Starred items do not need to be completed for an open show.

1 September	Show date
28 August	Prize cards and ring numbers made up
27 August	Catalogues collected or available
7 August	Final date for schedule and letters to all judges and helpers sent giving details of times, entries etc
1 August	Full details of times and entry to canine press★
21 July	Entry forms to printers
20 July	Closing of entries
20 June	Publication of schedule. Send 2 copies to the Kennel Club Show Department
7 June	Schedule announcement and adverts sent to canine press
7 May	Schedule complete and sent to printers
1 May	Copy of draft schedule sent to Kennel Club Show Department★
1 March	Orders for rosettes, prize cards etc complete
28 February	Last date for submission of judges already passed to award CCs to the Kennel Club. (Open shows do not have to submit the names of judges, but should still try to have them all appointed by this date)
28 February	Last date for applying for licence to run a championship show
31 December	Last date for submission of judges not already passed to award CCs★
1 December	All judges finalized as far as possible
1 October	Orders and bookings for benches, printer, tenting, showground/hall and catering completed.

For most championship shows judges should really be appointed at least twelve months prior to the show and the 'senior' judges, such as those for groups and best in show, at least two years prior to the show.

The time scale for an open show can be a good deal shorter than this, but the important thing is that a time scale is made out and kept to. Even though the deadlines are largely artificial, they are of considerable help and will avoid the last-minute rush and panic which, I am afraid, characterizes many minor dog shows.

Let us take each of the stages in detail. We have already discussed the initial application to run a dog show. This is included in the *Kennel Gazette* and returned immediately. After this the Kennel Club will send you the appropriate forms for the licence and this, too, should be returned as soon as possible.

By twelve months before the show, the committee should have decided on the venue and the secretary can then write the initial letters requesting services from caterers, benching and tenting contractors as well as actually booking the venue.

In the succeeding months judges should be selected and, where appropriate, questionnaires (obtained direct from the Kennel Club) should be sent to anyone who is to be appointed to award Challenge Certificates for the first time. Questionnaires must be with the Kennel Club nine months prior to the show at the very latest. Other judges all need to be 'approved' by the Kennel Club to award tickets, but only six months notice is required for these. Naturally, as approvals are received the judges must be informed by letter. Announcements are made in the *Kennel Gazette* of those approved, but it is polite to let people know what is happening. Open and other shows do not have these problems, of course. Their judges do not need Kennel Club approval, but the principle of informing all those involved is just as important.

By six months prior to the show all orders for rosettes, prize cards and any other specials and printing should be complete so that the decks are cleared for the production of the schedule.

The preparation of the schedule is not as complicated as it might first appear. There are hundreds of examples of content and layout available and most shows will be able to be based on the schedule produced the previous year. Nevertheless it is important to go through it carefully each year. Regulations change and so do committees, guarantors, venues and entry fees. Some rules printed in schedules are also unnecessary or outdated (I found a championship show schedule printed during the mid-seventies which contained a rule stating that dogs sent by rail should be 'in a strong box and provided with a stout chain'. Those rules cannot have been even looked at for many years for it is a very long time since shows would take on that responsibility!). The Kennel Club regulations state quite clearly what should be contained in the schedule and it would be pointless to list these here. However, there are one or two things sometimes forgotten and some pitfalls to avoid.

I keep a 'general' ring file devoted to each show, and another which is concerned solely with judges. The list of judges, copies of their invitations, their replies and notes of expenses and fees are all filed in schedule order. At the front is a complete list of breeds with a series of columns beside them giving the name of the judge, the date they were invited, the date they replied, whether or not they need a questionnaire, the date they were passed and a note of their fee. These details can

No wonder choosing the best puppy is so difficult. These Westies are like peas in a pod!

always be checked with the original documents, but it is handy to have them easily available when it comes to committee queries and drafting the schedule. Incidentally, when judges are invited a space is left asking them to say how they would like their name to appear in the schedule. Many judges could not care less, but some like to have just their initials, others their full name and some like their prefix to appear as well. It can save embarrassment, too. Some women judges are better-known under their maiden name and others like it to be clear whether they are Mrs, Miss or Ms.

In the 'general' file is the list of guarantors and all other correspondence with services being provided for the show and the Kennel Club. This information, plus the committee's decisions regarding the actual breeds and classes to be scheduled, is therefore all available and the secretary can combine it all on the schedule. Some secretaries type everything out afresh but most just modify last year's schedule. Show printers are quite used to this, but it must be done very carefully. Simple changes of names or numbers are relatively easy, but if a completely new breed and classification is introduced, it is much better to type it out on a separate sheet, put 'A' in the place you want it to appear and mark 'A' on the insert. You then send your inserts, clipped together in the correct order, along to the printer who will find it a lot easier to type or typeset the schedule.

Be careful about numbering: a change in the number of classes your society is scheduling for Afghan Hounds will change the class numbers throughout the schedule. This sounds obvious and easy to correct, but by the time you have inserted a number of other classes and turned over a page or two, it is easy to leave a gap in the numbering, or (which is much worse) two classes with the same number. It will give the secretary much more work in the long run if these details are not checked to start with.

Exactly which classes should be scheduled must be determined by the committee taking into account the entries of the previous year. As entries grow more classes are added, as they fall they are reduced or dropped altogether in favour of other breeds. This, of course, does not apply to championship shows where Challenge Certificates have been allocated by the Kennel Club. However small the entry, the society is expected to put those classes on.

When you have classes for more than one of Dachshunds, Poodles or Chihuahuas, it is sensible to send two entry forms and to put a note in the schedule that they should be entered on different forms. It causes enormous problems if exhibitors put the different breeds on the same form – it is not difficult to copy them out or get them photocopied, of course, but the time it takes can be a major headache.

It is usual to send a copy of the schedule to all those who exhibited at the show the previous year. A space is often left on the entry form for the exhibitors to fill in their names and addresses, so that this can be cut out and stuck on an envelope. It is very important that those schedules are sent out *before* the advertisements for the show appear. If they do not a great deal of time and money is wasted as regular exhibitors contact the secretary asking for a schedule and explaining that they ought to have received one. Some printers now have their catalogues set with the help of a computer and labels and reminders are made available automatically. This practice will obviously become more widespread in the future but, for the moment, I think it better to have all this information to hand.

Advertising

Apart from circulating last year's exhibitors, schedules can be sent to regular exhibitors of the breeds scheduled. This is a very time-consuming job, but can be worth it in some instances. Otherwise, secretaries rely on distribution at shows and on advertising in the canine press.

There are various views on advertisements for shows. Some believe that the simple bold advertisement is best, while others think that the maximum amount of information should be included. My personal opinion inclines towards maximum information, for my experience is that this reduces the number of postal and telephone queries during the busiest part of show management, the receipt and collation of entries. If only the venue and the name and address of the secretary are included in advertisements the telephone never stops ringing. I like to see breeds scheduled, number of classes and judges on an advertisement, as well as complete information regarding entry fees, car parking and membership of the society. In fact, some societies have introduced a code for their advertisements so that the individual classes are specified. This enables exhibitors to enter the show without having to send for a schedule at all and although this means marginally more work at the schedule stage, it saves a great deal in printing costs for schedules and in postage and telephone charges for both society and exhibitor.

Advertisements should be sent to the dog papers well in advance of the show and with the date(s) of insertion clearly specified. Some societies have their schedules out well in advance of closing of entries, others much later. I do not think it makes a significant difference to the entry and I try to stick to the time schedule listed on page 61.

Incidentally, if new breeds are being scheduled, it is as well to send a schedule to the breed note writers in the breed. A mention of the show will then be included here as well, although it is only fair to say that it may be edited out if the editor notices that they have not received any paid advertising for the show!

Occasionally, too, the schedule is not published separately but the whole of it is included in the canine press. This is an excellent method of wide distribution, but you have to be one of the very biggest societies for this to be cost-effective.

Prize Money

Until quite recently all societies paid prize money, but economic pressures during the seventies led several to discontinue this and now only a few championship shows offer prize money and many open shows have followed suit.

In terms of entries it does not seem to matter. Some committees believe very strongly that prize money should be retained – others take the opposite view. The original idea was to avoid increasing entry fees, although the present entry fee structure does not reflect this, some of the shows which have the highest entry fees being the ones who do not pay prize money.

Stewards and Other Helpers

Well before the show, arrangements for stewards and other assistants should be finalized. Larger shows usually have a chief steward and the best of these organizes both the appointment and allocation of stewards, just sending a complete list to the secretary for inclusion in the catalogue. At smaller shows this is often part of the secretary's work, although I personally see it as an aspect of show management so it is fully discussed under this heading. Mention is made of these vital helpers at this stage to emphasize their importance.

Stewards, car park attendants, catalogue sellers and other officials, whether they be members or friends of the society or professionals paid for their services, can make or break a show. They contribute to the general atmosphere from the time the show opens and if they are badly informed, harassed or overworked, it is both unfair on them and leaves a damaging impression in the mind of the exhibitor. On the other hand, if they are cheerful, welcoming and are able to be helpful, then the whole show benefits enormously. The greatest compliment a society can receive is 'Well, I haven't won, but I've enjoyed my day'.

Receipt of Entries and Preparation of Catalogue

The real work now begins. With any medium to large show there are constant telephone calls and letters asking for copies of the schedule and other information. A few entries arrive soon after the schedules

A typical morning's post the day after entries close for a big championship show. The dog looks askance – and so would you if you had to open and sort out that lot!

SOUTHERN COUNTIES CANINE ASSOCIATION

BREED _____ No of CLASSES _____ AV. per CLASS _____ SHEET No____

Name	Address	Cheque	P.O.	Cash	No of Dogs	No of entries	No of entries in stakes	Dogs entered in other breeds	No of entries in other breeds	Memb. S. J.	Car P.	Cara.	Ads	Overpaid Underpaid
TOTALS														

FIG. 5 Recording entries

have been distributed, but the bulk lands on the mat during the week before and the two or three days after the closing of entries. Over the years we have found the easiest way to deal with them is as follows:

1 Open the envelopes in batches and *pin* (not staple or paper clip) *everything* in the envelope to the entry form. (Always *look* into the envelope before it is thrown into the litter basket, as there is a tendency for a cheque or one of several postal orders to stick inside!)
2 Enter the details on the entry form on an analysis sheet (as illustrated). The cheques, postal orders and any cash should be removed at this stage. This gives a record which can be referred to quickly after the forms have been sent to the printers and is very useful for calculating, analysing and cross-checking your income from the show.
3 When the bulk of the entries has been received, sort into breeds, then into alphabetical order of exhibitors within the breeds. (Some printers now use computers and do not require the forms to be sorted at all. I thought initially that this was going to save a great deal of work, but in fact the sorting still has to be done as all entries need to be easily found at the show in the event of a query.)
4 Number.
5 Forward to printer.

We have found it best during the checking to put any queries to one side, in batches of the same sort of query, to be dealt with later. Each entry form needs to be checked to ensure that all the required information is included and that the money sent with the entry is correct. A note needs to be made on the entry form (we use a thick red pen) to indicate car parking pass, membership badge or catalogue voucher, if these are to be sent with passes by the printer although, as previously explained, most shows no longer send passes.

The queries can be divided into several groups:

1   Those forms which lack *essential* information. This includes everything from name and address to class numbers and generally the exhibitor must be contacted if the entry is to be included.
2   Those forms which lack some information such as the name and address for sending passes or the name of the breed or breeder. This can often either be copied in or looked up in a recent catalogue.
3   Forms which have two breeds. These must either be copied out completely by hand or photocopied.
4   Forms which are illegible.
5   Entry fees which have not been calculated correctly.
6   Forms which are inaccurate. These can be anything from a Golden Retriever entered in a class for Boxers to a two-year-old dog being entered in a puppy class.

Fortunately, the percentage of queries is quite low, but they can take up an enormous amount of time and money.

Before sending the completed and collated forms to the printer they should be grouped in breeds and placed in *schedule* order so that the class numbers run consecutively through the catalogue. Before each breed or group of breeds the name of the judge should be inserted and, if a championship show, whether or not Challenge Certificates are on offer. Full instructions should be given as to what regulations and information should be included. This often consists of an index, analysis of entries, map of the showground and times of judging.

There are two basic methods of compiling catalogues and how it is done depends largely on the printer you use. Most championship show catalogues print the names and addresses of the exhibitors followed by the dogs entered in the breed and their breeding and classes in a single list. Immediately afterwards come the class lists, which include the names of the dogs entered in each class. Dogs entering their first class are set in capital letters or bold type and dogs from previous classes in standard type. I believe this method is marginally cheaper in terms of paper consumption and more convenient, but many prefer to see the details of the dogs in the class together and the other method of compilation allows exhibitors to do this. In this method all the details of the dog, except the name and address of the owners, are included after the dog's name for the first class it is entered in. Dogs appearing in subsequent classes are just indicated by their names. The names and addresses of owners are then listed at the back of the catalogue.

I personally much prefer the first method as an exhibitor and judge, but also believe that it is technically more efficient for both secretary and printer.

Finally, firm arrangements must be made with the printer for the delivery of the catalogues when printed. As a general rule the number of catalogues required will be between one-third and one-half of the numbers of *dogs* entered. If I was running a show which had 500 dogs entered, I would therefore expect to order 200 catalogues, although I would be the first to admit that this is a particularly tricky decision for the cost of printing is high. It is wasteful to print too many catalogues but it reflects badly on the show management if there are not enough for all those that want them. My experience is that rather more catalogues are bought at general and group championship shows than at open shows.

Before the Show

Once the entry forms are sent to the printers, it is courteous to send a schedule to each of the judges with a note of the entry they have received (this is usually just written in beside the class numbers), directions to the show ground, a note of the time they need to arrive and whatever passes are necessary.

The secretary can now concentrate on the judges' envelopes and stewards' boxes. Each judge will need an envelope which should include:

Judging book
Judge's rosette or badge
Schedule
Challenge Certificates (if on offer)
Handwipers
Luncheon ticket(s) (preferably in separate envelope)
Details of wet weather arrangements (if the show is held outside)

It may also include reply-paid envelopes and letters from the canine press for their judges report, but these are occasionally sent direct to the judge.

Each ring will need a steward's box or bag, which should include:

Catalogue
Schedule
Prize cards and ring numbers (see below)
Rosettes and specials on offer
Details of judging, ring and weather accommodation (if the show is held outside)
Steward's report sheet (see illustration under exemption show description on p. 23)
Instructions to Stewards, as published by the Kennel Club

PRIZE CARDS AND RING NUMBERS

Each class should have its prize cards and the ring numbers of the dogs in that class held together by an elastic band. (Some societies who hold benched shows now distribute the bench numbers direct to the benches. This saves some time for the secretary, but numbers tend to get lost or forgotten, leading to confusion in the ring.) This is something of a last-minute job because it is convenient to wait until a copy of the catalogue is available. The printer should be asked to send a proof or copy of the catalogue as soon as it is ready. Two people working together is most convenient, one reading out the appropriate numbers from the catalogue and one picking them up in the correct order. As each class is finished, the numbers can be banded with a set of prize cards (on which the class number has previously been inserted). When each breed is completed, the whole set of classes can be banded and placed straight into the steward's bag.

If prize money is being paid at an open show, it is usually stapled (in an envelope if it is coin) to the prize card at this stage. Championship shows that pay prize money usually have a tear-off voucher on the prize card which is redeemable for the prize at the treasurer's office on the day of the show.

At this point the show secretary's work is completed and the show manager takes over. However, as previously stated, this is only a guideline and every society and committee is likely to have their own system and arrangements which are perfectly satisfactory. These will divide responsibilities and work in ways which best suit the show and the exhibitor.

Show Management

The position of show manager can be anything from a glorified errand boy to the leader of a successful team. The arrangements for a larger show are made many months in advance and even for a small show good

Putting on a championship show takes a lot of time and effort as can be seen from this photograph. Planning must be meticulous if it is to run smoothly. There looks as though there is plenty of room during the days before the show when only the tents are erected . . .

. . . But imagine the chaos if arrangements had not been made to accommodate all these cars, all these people and all these dogs

planning and clear thinking have a fundamental part to play if exhibitors, judges and helpers are to return home having had an enjoyable day.

Before becoming involved in the business of making the arrangements for dogs to be shown, it would be as well to introduce and discuss the 'three Cs'. In some ways they are the foundation upon which the show is built, because if they are not accorded the time and attention they deserve, they will certainly spoil the show. The three Cs are Car parking, Catering and Conveniences and their successful implementation is bound up primarily with the committee's choice of venue. Obviously, when venues are being considered, the first essential is adequate space for the dogs to be judged, but this is very closely followed by the three Cs; I feel that unless a committee is sure that most of these prime factors are better than adequate, it would be wise to seek another venue.

CAR PARKING

The majority of exhibitors arrive at a show by car or, in the case of general championship shows, by coach. Either way they have to move their dogs and the rest of their paraphernalia from car park to bench or ring. It is their first real contact with the show and the show management must have satisfactory answers to the following questions:

(a)   Is the car park (and therefore the show) easy to find? If not, what improvement should be made to directions or map in the schedule, or signposting on the day?
(b)   Is there likely to be a build-up of traffic at the entrance to the show? If so, what arrangements can be made to improve traffic flow? Incidentally, if a lot of cars are coming off a major road, police assistance is free.
(c)   Do cars park neatly and economically? If they do not, what improvements can be made?
(d)   Once out of their cars, do exhibitors have clear directions to get to the part of the show they need?
(e)   Once in, can exhibitors leave the car park easily? Some societies make a great effort to get people in and allow chaos to develop at the end of the show, although the relaxation of rules regarding times of attendance has largely alleviated this problem.

CATERING

At many small shows the catering is organized by members of the committee. This is often done on the bring-and-buy principle and there is no doubt that such an arrangement can make a considerable contribution to club funds. (If the catering is organized this way, then it should be made absolutely clear both in the schedule and on the entry form.) On the other hand, it does mean that a number of people are prevented from properly enjoying the show and this really does not seem fair as it is often the same people who are asked to do this job year after year. (The same could be said of committee members who organize the cups or a raffle, but at least they can feel part of the show!) Home-produced food is usually much better, too, but I have always argued that unless there is a member of the association who cheerfully volunteers for this duty and actually enjoys it, then an outside caterer should be called in.

Good-quality catering is yet another essential element. Those who are left to do it, whether volunteers or professionals, should be absolutely reliable, cheerful and competent. Nobody likes to queue or be served with unappetizing food or drink. Catering is one of those areas that is best sorted out and agreed well before the show. Leaving it until the last minute because so-and-so will probably do it is a short cut to chaos.

The use of local authority sports centres as venues for shows often means that the committee must use the facilities they provide and, unfortunately, the standard of service and the quality of their food is often very low. They are often crowded with wet children and unacceptably loud and healthy adults, too, so I view the use of such premises with considerable suspicion. However, if the show manager is prepared to negotiate hard, then the managers of such centres can usually be persuaded to arrange something better than that with which most users of sports centres are prepared to be satisfied!

The catering at open-air shows needs a good deal of thought. It is not just a question of a tent and a few tables. Provision must be made for people both in fine and, most importantly, in wet weather. The accommodation and the caterers must be considered in very great detail well before the show. There are plenty of good caterers who do an excellent job but it is always wise before booking them to visit a venue at which they are working. Once a company has been found who can really do the job then they are worth hanging on to; it is not worth chopping and changing for the sake of a few pounds. This is yet another area in which looking after the pence is often a false economy.

CONVENIENCES

The main problem with toilets is that people all want to use them at the same time. On arrival or immediately after lunch are not the times to choose to visit the conveniences at most shows if you are female. At some even the 'Gents' develops a queue, although it must be said that some shows do make a special effort or have a particularly well-served venue. The biggest problems are those outdoor shows which have to hire portable toilets, for they are expensive both in themselves and in the provision of tanks or piping.

We all tend to push the question of lavatories to the back of our minds, unless we actually need one, and there is a tendency to let the loos fend for themselves at a dog show. Certainly, it is often impossible to increase the capacity, but what is not impossible is at least to make them as civilized as possible, so that if people have to wait they do find soap, towels, toilet paper and litter bins stocked or emptied as the case may be.

It is here that the show management is seen to care about the exhibitors. It is not difficult to ensure before the show that the toilets are clean, that the locks work and the smallest rooms are well ventilated. It also takes very little time to freshen up the place and top up the consumables during the day, resulting in exhibitors feeling refreshed after their visit, rather than frustrated. Care in this area is one which pays real dividends, for some shows are known by the quality of their toilets and this really does modify the attitude of exhibitors. Every little thing that the committee does to make the life of the exhibitor easier reduces the pressure both on themselves, the dogs and the show management.

Complaints

The attitude of exhibitors is something over which the committee has only partial control. All the work that is put in to making the show pleasant and efficient can be completely destroyed if the heavens open. It matters not whether the venue is indoor or outdoor, the weather itself affects both exhibitor and management. On a fine day the secretary's table is calm, ordered and tranquil (most of the time, anyway), but if it is pouring with rain there is a queue of irate exhibitors all threatening to complain about something or other to the Kennel Club.

This is something that anyone involved in any organization and in the organization of dog shows in particular just has to get used to. Secretary, show manager, stewards and committee need to keep their tempers at all times for, in my experience, however 'right' you are, losing your cool only makes matters worse.

My own approach when anyone is 'difficult' and demands their 'rights' is not to argue. The simplest, and quickest solution, is to say that they can do whatever they want but, naturally, it will be put in the secretary's report of the show to the Kennel Club and that they will sort the matter out. Never try to convince someone that they are wrong: it only leads to unnecessary confrontations.

The sort of problems that arise usually concern whether or not a particular dog could, or should, be entered in a class, whether it can transfer to another class, whether the exhibitor and dog are allowed to leave the showground or whether particular winners are allowed to withdraw from classes under special circumstances.

These requests are not the same as those complaining about the organization of the show itself, the behaviour of another exhibitor or the procedure or the placings of a judge. All such complaints *must* be referred to the Kennel Club. They can be done at the show or later but to be considered they must be in writing and must be accompanied by the appropriate fee (currently £5.00).

One perennial request is from the exhibitor who arrives late and misses a class. The Kennel Club show regulations are quite clear on this: a dog may only be transferred to another appropriate class if it has been entered in a class which specifies a different sex, a different colour (within the breed), or if it is a puppy entered in a minor puppy class. If an *appropriate* class is not scheduled, or there is any other reason for the dog being ineligible (too old for puppy or Junior or entered in Graduate having done too much winning for the class) then it must be transferred to the Open class. If an exhibitor *misses* a class, it is not eligible to go into the Open class. If the exhibitor insists on showing the dog, then I would allow him or her to do so but, of course, the circumstances would have to be reported to the Kennel Club, along with details of any prizes won, plus the details of any dogs that would have been placed had the offending exhibit been absent.

The important thing to remember is that the exhibitor is under as much stress as you are so – for the sake of the show and the other people around – do keep calm! The same, of course, applies to everyone on the show. Keep everything under control and if problems arise bring them up at the first committee meeting after the show (at Southern Counties, we have a specific 'post mortem' meeting, when we review the whole show). Anything not remembered by that time was probably due to temporary stress in any case! It saves a lot of trouble at the show, anyway.

Stewards and Stewarding

The world of show dogs is fortunate that so many people are prepared to give freely of their time to be the link between the show manager, the exhibitor and the judge. They are an extremely important body of men and women, some of whom are interested only in their own breed, some in learning about dogs generally and a few who just enjoy a day out with dogs and dog people. Whatever their motives, they should be assiduously cosseted by the show manager, for without them the show would not run at all.

As with everything else, it is sensible to organize stewards well in advance. Some of the bigger shows have a chief steward, who takes on the responsibility of organizing all the stewards, from contacting them

Throughout judging the steward keeps an eye on what is going on so that all placings are carefully recorded. Here Arthur Brown is checking a point with an exhibitor while Jean Lanning, in the background, is making notes on the dogs

in the first place to placing them in the appropriate rings, as well as actually issuing them with their various cards, numbers, catalogues, etc on the day of the show.

However, most show secretaries and managers do the administrative work connected with the organization of stewards and the chief steward just organizes the stewards in the day. 'Just' is really the wrong word here, because a good chief steward can take an enormous load off the shoulders of both the show manager and secretary and can make a significant contribution to the smooth running of the show.

These three – secretary, show manager and chief steward – are a small sub-committee which should meet, sometimes with the chairman and one or two other committee members or friends, to plan the timing of the show. When the entries are closed and the numbers of dogs are known, a reasonable estimate of how long everything should take can be made.

The actual running order of the show is usually fixed well in advance and depends greatly on the number of rings available and what breeds and varieties are being judged by what judges. However, there should always be a disclaimer on the schedule to the effect that the running of the show order may be altered, although, of course, it is essential that breeds advertised as starting later than the opening of the show should not be begun earlier than the stated time. On the other hand there is still some flexibility and if there is any possibility of using rings more effectively, it should be used, as nothing disconcerts exhibitors more than hanging around an empty ring waiting to be judged.

When the decisions have been made a clear list of rings and approximate times should be made and displayed at the secretary's table or at some other convenient site for the exhibitors. Shows that send out passes often take the opportunity to send exhibitors a sheet showing the timetable, map of the areas and a map of the venue itself, and this is an excellent idea. There will always be questions for the show organizers, of course, but the more confident and clear the exhibitors are about where they should be, the more they will feel that the show has their interests at heart. Everybody has a more enjoyable day as a result.

On a personal note I find that when talking to show secretaries, managers and stewards, I am amazed at the number, at all levels, who view their exhibitors as a nuisance. We all have our stories which show how easy it is for novices to get things hopelessly wrong, but I can see no point in taking on these tasks unless they are fundamentally enjoyable. Certainly, any advantages that exhibitors feel are gained by being the officer of a canine association are largely illusory so what benefit such people gain from the position I cannot imagine!

The specific tasks of ring stewards are laid out in the relevant Kennel Club Regulations. Some believe that it is their task to control the ring, but this is not so. Control of the ring is the responsibility of the judge; the steward is there to help and assist both judge and exhibitors and to ensure that the various demands of the Kennel Club Regulations are met.

The inexperienced judge will receive considerable help from an experienced ring steward. The pressures on judges in the ring are considerable and it is very easy to make a mistake by lining up the dogs the wrong way or even not examining an exhibit that, perhaps, arrives late and is not positioned in the correct place. The good steward will be aware of this sort of problem and be able to tactfully direct the judge's attention to anything that may cause difficulty. By the same token, the officious and self-important steward can cause chaos by trying to do the judge's organization for him. I believe that all exhibitors benefit from stewarding regularly and certainly it is a very helpful experience for the prospective judge.

In the ring the steward should ensure that exhibitors are aware that the classes have begun and this is particularly important if the classes do not start after the official commencement of judging.

The steward should:

Mark up the class numbers on the ring award board.

Give out ring numbers to exhibitors if they have not already got
them.
Having consulted with the judge, position exhibitors and handlers in
the ring.
Keep an eye on the ringside for instances of people attracting dogs
being shown.
Give out awards after the judge has placed the exhibits.
Keep a record of the placings on the steward's sheet on the ring
award board and the judge's catalogue.
Stick up the ring award board slip.

Many stewards accept responsibility for getting seen dogs into the ring
in the right order for this can be quite complicated in variety classes.
The stewards should always consult with the judge prior to the class so
that they are both using the same criteria. For instance, some judges
like all the dogs which have not been placed before the other dogs they
have seen, even if those dogs are the first-prize winners. Other judges
prefer that the winners of, say, Open be placed before the winner of
Limit, even if the second prize in the Open class is still in the ring.

It is easy to say that a judge ought to be able to remember placings and
dogs and that if he has judged them he should come up with the same
conclusions in the next class. However, not only are the differences
often marginal between dogs placed consecutively (especially lower
down the line), but if the judge is to concentrate on the dogs in front of
him, it is all too easy for a flashy dog to take his eye as he is making the
placings, which had he had the time and the opportunity to go over and
watch again, would not be placed as highly. The steward, therefore, has
a considerable responsibility, both to the judge and the exhibitor.

Judging also requires considerable concentration and, as already
mentioned, a judge, although aware of the correct rules and procedures,
can often make mistakes. The best stewards will quietly intervene to
correct the error. Judges often ask specific questions about procedures,
too, so stewards must have a good working knowledge of the show's
and the Kennel Club's rules.

Despite all the administration and planning, show management must
still be flexible. Just because a decision has been taken and approved
does not mean that an alternative solution might not be an improvement
or that mistakes may not have been made. The show manager should
have authority from the committee to make adjustments to the site and
to the running order, if appropriate – so long as it does not contravene
any of the Kennel Club's Rules, of course. There is nothing worse for
exhibitors than to be hanging around for judging with several empty
rings available. Naturally, this may happen in, say, a lunch break, but
if a ring is finished with, there is no reason at all why breeds should not

be placed in it if their own ring is still being used. By the same token, if a ring is too small and can be enlarged, then it should not need a committee meeting to take such a decision. It is the job of the show manager and chief steward to ensure that such things are done.

A beautiful Basenji head showing the typical expression of the breed

On the Day

In theory, if all the arrangements have been properly made little should be required of the secretary 'on the day'. However, it is important that both secretary and show manager should not be tied down to any specific job. At small shows there is a tendency for them to offer to help with the refreshments, the raffle and selling catalogues! The good committee has all these jobs properly covered and there will be plenty for the secretary and show manager to do without getting involved in tasks which will distract them from their overall responsibility for the smooth running of the show. Both must be available to answer questions, to resolve problems and to generally make exhibitors welcome.

How much work needs to be done on the site before the show begins depends very much on the venue and the size of the show. The more that is done for you by the contractors and the staff of the venue, the greater will be the cost, so it is sensible for the committee and members to do as much as possible. Once again, we return to the basic principles that everyone should know what is required of them and have clear instructions about their jobs. There is no need for these to be officious or demanding and I try to write a personal letter to those in charge of each section, setting out their areas of responsibility and asking them to contact me if they have any queries. Even then there are points of misunderstanding, but these can usually be picked up and dealt with quickly if everything else is planned.

Throughout the day a careful watch should be kept on the timing of the show. If the entry exceeds previous numbers by very much, then the committee should already have made provision for this by, say, increasing the number of rings, or (exceptionally) beginning the show and the judging of some breeds earlier than that stated in the schedule. However, the timing might still be out and it is important to take decisions early in the day if one of the judges is much slower than expected or the start of judging is delayed by someone being late.

Even the smallest show can be both friendly, enjoyable and 'professional'. In fact, a show run really well stands a much greater chance of being enjoyed by all, because there are no quarrels and no panics!

Unfortunately, at all levels there are some who lose badly. By its very nature, showing dogs excites our competitive instincts and because judging is a matter of opinion rather than fact, there are ample opportunities for disagreement. A proportion of these have to be faced by the secretary or show manager and, in my experience, it is better to suggest that the matter is referred to the Kennel Club than to take sides – unless, of course, it is a simple matter of a mistake which can be easily cleared up. Those that take on the task of running shows ought to get a great deal of pleasure and satisfaction from their success but, as with every job, there are aspects of it that are less pleasant and this is one that comes as part of the package. Those few exhibitors who do make everyone's life difficult are fortunately only a small percentage.

Properly organized, a dog show should almost run itself. Left to itself, it can be, and sometimes is, total chaos.

A Word about Trade Stands

At the bigger shows 'the Trade' turn out in force. I welcome them, although I am afraid that there are some who consider them a necessary nuisance. I believe that the trade stands are a colourful backdrop to the show and make a real contribution to it, both in the fees they pay for their space and the service they enable the show to offer exhibitors.

The 'hard core' of the Trade comprises forty to fifty stands, with a much smaller group of short-lived traders who try the circuit and give up quite quickly. They, too, are in competition and at a new venue there is considerable negotiation and jockeying for the best position. However hard the show manager tries, there are always some who are dissatisfied, but by and large, the trade-stand holders, some of whom are employed by large companies but many of whom are self-employed, are a marvellous and cheerful group who work well together and are prepared to give anyone a hand.

In planning for trade stands, the show manager needs to know the numbers very early on. Some of the larger shows have quite a long waiting list, while others have enough space to fit everyone in.

A plan of the ground showing the site of each stand must be circulated well before the show and those with large vehicles must expect to be in place in plenty of time. Most standholders have their own stand – often part of a caravan or a specially designed display and sales unit – although some will require a tent which they must pay the show for on top of the site fee. Site fees vary widely, but are usually based on a 'foot frontage' fee. Some shows work out their fees on a square metre basis, others have a basic ground rent plus a 'foot frontage' fee. Naturally, the shows which have the largest entries and the biggest public 'gate' tend to charge more than the smaller shows.

Many of the self-employed traders also take their stand to local open shows when not on the championship show circuit. Stand fees are cheap at these shows and, so long as there are only one or two present, then their turnover at these events can be quite respectable.

To Sum Up

I suppose there are areas of activity that require a wider range of skills and even more tact than that of running the average dog show, but I cannot think of any! It is a job that has to be done before the difficulties and work level can be appreciated, but for those of us who receive satisfaction from seeing the miriad pieces of an organized human and canine jigsaw coming together to form an enjoyable, cohesive whole, it is a source of considerable pleasure.

It is a field, too, which is wide open. With something like 1500 canine societies and breed clubs, there is a constant demand for enthusiasts who have organizing ability and love dogs to serve on committees and to run, or help in the running of, dog shows. Unfortunately, there is no official training for canine society secretaries, it is another one of those things which is learnt from experience. On the other hand, there are plenty of other secretaries and committee members who will be pleased to help. They usually only need to be asked and, although this is sometimes difficult to begin with, it gets easier when it is realized that people like to help and advise.

After the Show

The Lord Mayor's Show and dog shows have very much the same problem – there is a great deal of clearing up to do. Most of it is sheer hard work, but there is plenty for the secretary and treasurer too.

The secretary's primary duty is to report any complaints or problems to the Kennel Club, along with a marked catalogue. For an open show this is quite straightforward, but for a championship show the secretary's report (which will include everything from a list of people who have been given permission to leave early to the names and circumstances of dogs which have been moved from one class to another) can be several typewritten pages.

Occasionally, there is something more serious. An exhibitor may complain about the way in which a class has been judged or (after the allocation of a prize) inform the secretary that the dog was not eligible for the class for some reason. In almost every circumstance no action should or need be taken by the show management, other than to report the matter to the Kennel Club. I know that I have emphasized this point before, but I make no apology: exhibitors occasionally allow themselves to get very excited and it is much the best policy not to argue, accept everyone's word that what has been said is true (because, after all, they certainly think that it is) and report the matter in full.

Everything that has to be done is listed in the Kennel Club's Regulations concerning various shows. These are not always easy to interpret and it is important that those running shows are prepared to contact the Kennel Club Show Department to ask. There should be no problem about this. The Show Department, and the Kennel Club for that matter, is there to serve the interests of dogs and the rules are there to try to provide a working structure within which people can show dogs effectively. Occasionally, the regulations are up-dated to cope with changing circumstances, but most have stood the test of time and the Show Department is always willing to help canine societies.

I believe that it is important to thank people. Most of the work that goes into running a show is voluntary and even if it is not, there is no reason not to be grateful for services which have helped the show to be successful. A postcard is usually quite sufficient for only an acknowledgement of their participation and thanks for their contribution are required. It makes for better public relations and this will ensure that your helpers are happy to be involved next time.

After the show a post-mortem committee meeting should be held. However successful the show, there is always room for improvement and I always find I have quite a long list from my own committee of things which must be attended to for the following year. The organization breaks down sometimes, too. If you have had a disaster and the caterer provided for fifty rather than five hundred or no toilet paper was available after eleven o'clock because the groundsman or caretaker had gone off duty, then the responsibility must be apportioned. It might be the fault of the show manager for not ensuring something was exactly understood or a company that did not properly fulfil its contract. But to be honest, there is little that can be done if one of your voluntary helpers makes a minor mistake. Major errors of commission or omission may, of course, lead to resignation or removal if the office is one of election, but generally this is not the case. The committee learns from experience which people need to be reminded and encouraged. Voluntary help is required so the problems which accompany such help must be accepted. Over a period of years, secretaries and show managers build up teams on which they know they can rely.

If the problem was caused by a supplier of services, then the matter can be drawn to their attention, a proportion of their invoice not paid and, in the last resort, another company appointed to do the job. The important thing is to identify the problems and take whatever action is necessary to correct them for the future. I always photocopy the minutes of our post-mortem committee meeting and put in the front of my next year's file. Ideas and suggestions brought up during the year can also be added and acted on as necessary.

I now intend to indulge in a spot of philosophy, but it cannot be helped. It is important.

Training Classes, Seminars and Other Canine Activities

I believe that all canine societies have a responsibility that is wider than just running shows. For this reason I think they should all make some contribution to their breed or to the community in the form of meetings or training classes and, of course, many canine societies are very active in these areas. This is not only educationally and culturally important, but it also has a practical value. The exhibitors, breeders and judges of the future need to be attracted to the world of show dogs and they need to be helped and encouraged if they are to fulfil their potential. Therefore every organization must play its part in ensuring that the show dogs of the future are better in quality, more acceptable throughout the community and cared for to higher standards. Britain has an incredible and very rich canine heritage, which is woven into the fabric of our culture and must be preserved and developed.

Those of us who in some small way are involved in the organization and administration of the world of dogs carry an important responsibility and we have a duty to the companions that give so much to our lives to encourage and help people and their dogs throughout the community.

These objects are best achieved by local canine and training societies

Education for breeders and judges is most important. Joan Joshua, a well-known breeder of Chow Chows and a past lecturer at Liverpool School of Veterinary Medicine, regularly lectures on the anatomy and conformation of the dog, using a live model in the shape of her own Chow and a less live one in the shape of Fergus the skeleton!

encouraging responsible pet ownership in the first instance. With luck, those who are taught to look after their dogs properly will be encouraged to purchase a pedigree dog in the future and be involved in the world of shows and, in the long term, the improvement or establishment of their chosen breed.

In fact, almost every canine society has as one of its aims and objects a clause which states that the society has been formed to promote and establish a breed or further the interests of pedigree dogs. Many societies do not take this facet of their activities seriously and it would make a significant contribution to the community's attitude to dogs if they did so.

It is not the place of this book to go into details as to the way in which this could best be done. Every society has among its members those who have expertise in both presentation and organization. Most only need the opportunity and should be encouraged to develop this aspect of the society's activities.

In the long run, it can only be good for all of us in the world of show dogs.

4 Judging

I often wonder why people want to judge. It is a difficult task to begin with, apart from the fact that it takes you away from home, puts you in the centre of a ring in all weathers and ensures that you only satisfy a small proportion of the people who enter under you at the show. However, one might just as well ask why people show dogs in the first place. Nevertheless, there always seem to be plenty of exhibitors and plenty of judges. In fact, to be honest, many people feel that they are ready to judge long before they actually know enough to be able to give anyone a worthwhile and sensible opinion.

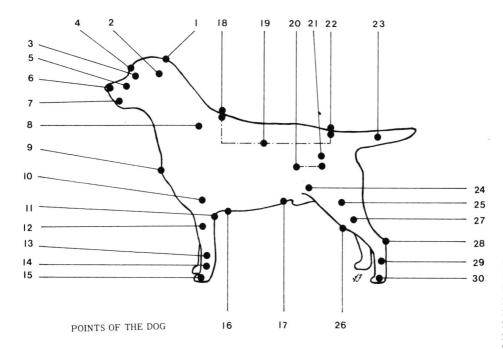

POINTS OF THE DOG

Length is measured from point of shoulder to point of buttock
Height is measured from withers to the ground

FIG. 6
POINTS OF THE DOG

1	Occiput
2	Ear
3	Eye
4	Stop
5	Muzzle
6	Nose
7	Mouth
8	Shoulder
9	Point of Shoulder
10	Upper Arm
11	Elbow
12	Forearm
13	Wrist
14	Pastern
15	Paw
16	Brisket
17	Tuck up
18	Withers
19	Back
20	Coupling
21	Loins
22	Croup
23	Tail
24	Flank
25	Thigh
26	Stifle
27	Second Thigh
28	Hock
29	Pastern
30	Paw

KEY TO MAJOR MUSCLES

A   Trapezius
B   Deltoids
C   Triceps
D   Pectoral
E   Extensor
F   Gluteal
G   Latissimus Dorsi
H   Sartorius
I   Biceps Femoris
J   Semitendinosius
K   Gastrocnemius

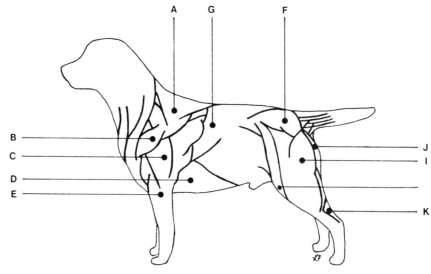

FIG. 7   MAJOR MUSCLES OF THE DOG

KEY TO SKELETON

A   Skull
B   Atlas
C   Axis
D   Scapula
E   Humerus
F   Ribs
G   Sternum
H   Radius
I   Ulna
J   Carpus
K   Metacarpus
L   Phalanges
M   Cervical vertebrae
N   Dorsal vertebrae
O   Lumbar vertebrae
P   Sacral vertebrae
Q   Coccygeal vertebrae
R   Pelvis
S   Femur
T   Tibia
U   Fibula
V   Patella
W   Tarsus
X   Metatarsus
Y   Phalanges

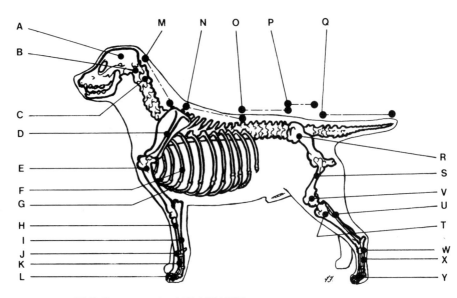

FIG. 8   SKELETON OF LABRADOR

Over the past 130 years or so, judges have been appointed by canine societies for all sorts of reasons. The main reason is, naturally, that the person has had considerable experience and success in that particular breed. On the other hand, they may have established themselves as a judge of another breed or of many other breeds and the committee of a breed club may feel that they have both the experience and the knowledge to make a worthwhile contribution. We may just as well clearly establish the difference between these two before we go any further.

The specialist judge normally has an intimate and detailed knowledge of the breed that he or she owns. They will have studied the breed in depth, they will have a very clear idea of the things that they like about the breed, and they will have a clear idea of the particular types of dog within the breed that they prefer. Their conception of what the breed should look like is usually very precise and they will be looking for dogs which approach this ideal as nearly as possible. The all-rounder, on the other hand, will not have such a detailed knowledge of the breed and will, therefore, approach the whole business of judging from a different direction. It may mean that his opinions and those of specialist breeders may not coincide - and they very often do not! The reason for this is that the all-rounder will almost certainly have a greater concern for other aspects of dogs than breed type.

Judy de Casembroot makes a careful examination of the fabulous Fresno at Richmond Championship Show. The handler is Geoff Corish

These other aspects will include overall conformation and angulation (we will get onto the discussion of these details later) and, most importantly, the original purpose of the breed as well as its soundness and movement. His different emphasis makes for a good deal of argument and discussion among breeders as to the value of specialists and all-round judges. Personally, I believe that both are a valuable asset when a breed is being judged. Some breeds refuse, almost point blank, ever to have all-round judges and to be honest, dogs in those breeds are often of less good quality than those who regularly come under the scrutiny of somebody who is more concerned with the overall physical look and power of the breed than they are in length of leg, shape of eye, set of ear, carriage of tail and so on. Either way, the all-rounder is an established figure within the world of show dogs in the United Kingdom and, in practice, very often gains much higher entries than specialists do when they come to judge.

Becoming a Judge

At one time, whenever a judge was proposed by a canine society for an open or championship show, the judge's name had to be submitted to the Kennel Club before they were actually allowed to go into the ring. This meant that the Kennel Club exercised a great deal of control over which judges were allowed to judge at the licensed shows (that is the open and the championship shows). Because dog shows became so much more popular during the fifties and sixties, this practice was dropped and now only championship show judges have to be 'approved' by the Kennel Club. What happens is that the championship show committee writes to the prospective judge and asks them to judge. (We have already discussed the methods of actually doing this in the previous section of this book.) On receiving such an invitation, the prospective judge, if they have not previously awarded Challenge Certificates in that particular breed, has to ask the society to send a questionnaire.

Questionnaires have been designed by the Kennel Club to try and sort out exactly what experience a prospective judge has. The form sent asks for the number of classes and the number of dogs that have been judged by the prospective judge in that particular breed, the names of the shows at which those classes were judged, what other breeds and varieties the prospective judge has done in the past and other information regarding their understanding of the world of dogs. On completion, the questionnaire is returned to the committee who examine it to make sure that the person they have asked to judge is, in fact, competent, and then it is sent to the Kennel Club where it is examined by the Judges Sub-Committee. The Judges Sub-Committee may well ask breed societies whether or not they feel that person has the experience to judge the breed and when they have received the replies they come to a conclusion and inform the inviting canine society whether or not that person has been 'passed'.

Championship show committees select the judges in two ways. They either refer directly to the judging lists which are produced by the breed clubs, doing no more than sticking in a pin, or they ask their committees to research within the breed that is being discussed to see whom exhibitors would support. What the latter boils down to is that judging appointments depend largely on reputation. As yet there are no official Kennel Club examinations which say whether or not a person is a good judge. Personally, I believe that this will come, but for the moment the only opportunities for those who wish to judge dogs to learn formally is at breed club seminars or by taking the Judging Diploma Course run by the Canine Studies Institute. However, in the final analysis, it depends on experience and how well the individual is known within the breed that they wish to judge.

Another trio, this time of Rough Collie puppies

This experience is gained through the effort that the candidate puts in within his or her breed and into the world of dogs in general. There are three important basic requirements that anyone who accepts a judging appointment should be able to fulfil. They are in no particular order and are of equal importance. The first is to actually own and show very good dogs. (It helps if good dogs are bred, too, but it is being surrounded by the best that improves ones understanding of the term 'quality' in any breed.) The second is to have the skill to be able to assess quality. This is a talent and you either have it or you have not – it cannot be learned or taught, although, of course, it can be developed by thought and by study. If any of the three is to be put over the other two then having an 'eye' for a dog is probably the one. The third requirement is knowledge and, of course, this is where the development of expertise can be continually improved. There is a limit to the number of good dogs one can own and talent is, unfortunately, a constant in the equation but knowledge can always be increased and developed and it is a poor judge who believes that he has learned all there is to know.

There is a further quality that is required and it is one which, if it is lacking, can nullify any amount of talent, experience and expertise. This is integrity. Judging dogs is, essentially, a matter of opinion and those opinions vary enough for judges to be able to favour one dog above another for unacceptable reasons. When this happens, and it does occasionally, it is extremely difficult to prove and therefore any judge of quality puts his reputation for fair dealing above anything else. By the same token, a judge must be tough, too, for there will be plenty of people anxious to imply that he is dishonest if they are given half a chance.

There are, of course, other necessary qualifications but I should like to come back to those after further consideration of the three basic requirements already referred to, for I believe that we can take the necessity for integrity and strength of character without any disagreement.

LIVING WITH GOOD DOGS

Most people who are asked to judge have usually made some sort of impression within their breed, either because they have won consistently or have been generous with their time in helping a breed or general canine society. The world of dogs requires a constant supply of administrators and workers as well as of exhibitors, and anyone who stays the course for three or four seasons begins to be known within their breed and within their locality. However, it is possible to win and to work without absorbing the correct elements which go to make up 'quality' within a breed. The most obvious problem is that if an exhibitor only has one or two dogs (if two, they are often of very similar breeding in any case), they absorb information about those animals uncritically without consciously comparing them with dogs of better type. Our own dogs become the norm against which other animals are compared instead of being seen as one section of a large spectrum. The popular name for this condition is 'kennel blindness' and it is easy to spot in other people but not so easy to recognize in oneself!

The aspiring judge must recognize early in his career that his first-hand experience of dogs under general conditions is extremely limited and it is for this reason that, however intelligent and sensible a novice exhibitor is, his opinion will not usually be considered seriously by experienced exhibitors for several years. It is therefore essential that those dogs which are owned by aspiring judges should be of the very finest type and quality and that conscious attempts are made to see and examine critically dogs of established breeders and exhibitors other than the kennel from which their own stock was purchased. Having to choose puppies, too, is a salutary exercise and hones the edge of one's perception. I believe that breeders should do their best to see as adults all the puppies that they have bred and to have photographs and notes about them if they are to produce dogs of better quality. By the same token, a prospective judge can gain considerable experience in this way and the understanding gained can be very valuable.

Catherine Sutton, one of our most respected judges, examines a Swedish Vallhund at the Nordic Show

AN 'EYE' FOR A DOG

The ability to be able to assess and quantify 'quality' and the appreciation of symmetry, style and 'balance' is an inborn characteristic. Not to have this capacity is the visual equivalent of being tone deaf; if the innate skill or talent is not built in there is nothing that can be done about it. However, few people are born totally without the ability to make aesthetic judgments and if there is a spark it can be developed. I sometimes feel that some of our judges take considerable pride in putting out their spark, but that is something we all learn to put up with! The development of innate talent is only achieved by determination and by hard work. There are in dogs, as in any activity, a fortunate few who are brilliant – who have supreme talent – but, for most of us, what we have has to be nurtured and protected if it is to flower. This brings me on to the third necessity.

These days many judges use small tape recorders to dictate their reports rather than spending time writing them down. Here at Crufts the judge is commenting on the Lhasa Apsos. After each class the judge usually makes notes on the winners so that accurate reports can be written

KNOWLEDGE

The knowledge required by judges for any breed of dog is enormous. We shall consider its applications later but, for the present, I should just like to consider the two basic areas which must be properly understood by every judge. The first is information that is common to all dogs: this includes the history and development of canis familiaris, a knowledge of canine anatomy, an understanding of the basic mechanics of movement, an ability to define and assess temperament, an understanding of the role of the handler and, in the case of many breeds, a knowledge of what can be done by the experienced trimmer. It also includes experience of the actual business of organizing a ring, the routine which is expected by exhibitors, the completion of a judging book and the techniques of report writing – the list seems endless.

The second area is that of the breed or breeds being judged. Naturally, several of the earlier points will have a bearing on breed type – particular breeds have individual actions, for instance, and it is sometimes difficult to determine where the development of the dog in general becomes the development of a particular breed. However, a thorough understanding of breed type plus the ability to interpret the standards of the breed are absolutely essential. This is not just a matter of learning the standard by heart. The standards are often referred to as 'the blueprint of the breed'. This is a very poor analogy because a blueprint implies accuracy in measurement and consistency in reproduction. Dogs are living creatures so, of course, any attempt to produce them as a series of absolutely identical types is doomed to failure. Furthermore, a blueprint implies completeness and finality. There are few breeds of which one can say that they are perfect; there must be room for manoeuvre if a breed has a potential for improvement. I prefer to see the standards as defining limits within which there is room for development – an artist's impression rather than a finished drawing or a photograph.

Naturally, the understanding and knowledge required of the judge is much greater than if he or she merely has to take measurements. A qualitative assessment is much more difficult when various characteristics have to be balanced one against the other in conjunction with the breed itself and those points made under our first heading.

These three necessities – talent, experience and knowledge – will, of themselves, give a judge another essential quality, that of confidence. I have already mentioned integrity and determination but confidence is, from the exhibitor's point of view, almost as important for there is nothing worse than watching a judge who is unable to come to a decision.

Decision-making is a skill all of its own and one which must be exercised with great care. A judge must tread the line between being decisive and being hesitant. If he works too quickly he will be accused of not taking enough care, if too slowly, of not knowing what he is doing. In the final analysis skill, knowledge and experience combine to produce a judge who has a clear idea of what the standard requires and who has the trust of breeders and of exhibitors. It takes a long time and a great deal of hard work.

Judging Procedures

Throughout this book I have been concerned with principles, procedures and practice rather than theory. Therefore, rather than go further into a complex discussion of judging theory I believe that a clearer picture will emerge if I go through the way in which a judge is appointed, carries out his appointment and writes it up afterwards. On the way we should also pick up a few pointers as to the approaches used and the background required by the prospective judge. For those who need more information there are several books (essential reading in any case) which go into considerable detail about every aspect of judging procedure. This book is not intended as a handbook for judges, but there is no doubt that an understanding of the way in which a judge works and of the varied ideas that have to be taken into consideration is most helpful to both exhibitors and to prospective canine society officials as well as to the potential judge himself.

Judges of experience regularly receive requests by telephone or by post to judge breeds or varieties from canine societies. Such requests should be answered quickly by letter as follows:

'Further to your letter (telephone call) I am pleased that I am able to accept (sorry that I am unable to accept) your kind invitation to judge Abyssinian Hoghounds and Varieties at Goole CA Open Show on Saturday 15 April. Please convey to your committee my sincere thanks (my sincere regrets). I look forward to further details and a copy of your schedule when available. I will be pleased to judge in an honorary capacity. (My fee and expenses will be £??.00.) Yours sincerely, etc.'

Note that the letter has specified the canine society, the date, the breeds and whether or not the appointment has been accepted. Also indicated is the expectation of further information and that a remuneration (or not) has been agreed. A *copy* of the letter should be made and kept safely in a file. The date should also be noted in a diary.

The question of fees is very difficult. Many people are pleased to judge for nothing and many canine societies do not expect to pay their judges. This is fine if the judge can afford it and certainly many active and potential all-round judges are pleased to officiate for new breeds at open show level for nothing just to get the experience. Unfortunately, it is an attitude which actually prevents some judges who have a great deal to offer ever being able to judge. I believe that canine societies must be prepared to pay reasonable fees and expenses if requested and I rather resent invitations which clearly indicate that the appointment 'will be in an honorary capacity'. I believe that the judge is the one best able to decide whether or not he can afford to travel and judge for nothing. The labourer (and that includes judges) is worthy of his hire.

In theory, the judge's reply should be at least acknowledged but it is quite usual for there to be no further communication until after the closing of entries when a schedule usually arrives with a note of the entry along with any other details, such as times of judging, car park pass and map etc, that may be relevant.

The good judge starts for the show allowing plenty of time in hand. There is nothing worse than for the judge to arrive at the ring ten minutes late and out of breath because there was a queue of traffic at the gate. On arrival the judge should report to the secretary who will provide details of the day plus a judging book, badge or rosette and a steward. The real work now begins.

IN THE RING

Before judging commences it is important to arrange with the steward exactly where exhibitors are to stand, to check that the table is stable and decide where seen dogs are going to stand. It also helps if a positive decision is taken as to where the winning dogs are going to be placed in the ring. All these conclusions must be compatible with the needs of the dogs and exhibitors – they, after all, are the ones who have paid.

There are two other practices that are traditional rather than useful. The first is the ring procedure which begins with all the handlers being asked to move round the ring with their dogs before the judge starts individual examinations. Personally, I feel that this is a pointless procedure unless the ring is really large, that it makes little contribution to judging and that it leads to an untidy and disorganized ring. However, there are others who believe that it allows dogs time to settle and every judge must make up their own mind. The other practice is the 'circular shuffle' where each handler and dog goes to the end of the line and everyone gradually moves around the ring. There is much to be said, particularly in a large class, for the procedure which brings each dog out to the centre of the ring and then returns it to the same place. The important thing, of course, is that the judge is consistent in the ring and that both steward and exhibitors know exactly what is happening.

I hope this shows that it is essential for a judge to work to a well-established routine. Apart from ensuring that no part of the procedure is missed it also helps exhibitors to know what to expect. Those that are experienced will then be able to approach at the right time and from the right direction and stand in the right place. A routine, too, increases the judge's confidence and the confidence of the exhibitors in the judge and this is bound to lead to more efficient and competent judging.

The examination of each individual dog is the single most important aspect of judging. The examination must be both gentle and thorough and it also needs to be extremely rapid. Each exhibit can be afforded about one and a half minutes of the judge's time and, if the classes are big, it might be closer to thirty seconds. The judge must know precisely what he is doing if the assessment is to be carried out completely and efficiently. Here is a suggested routine although, of course, there are variations:

1   The handler must be allowed to 'set up' the dog. Some breeds are shown 'stacked', ie set-up in a particular position. There are advantages

in this: some comparisons are much easier if the proportions of each dog can be directly compared and, particularly with those breeds with a long upper thigh, the position of the feet can significantly alter the conformation of the dog. Tail lengths, set and feathering can also be more easily compared if they are not waving madly about. On the other hand, a good handler can disguise faults by careful adjustments. The hand holding the head can take up surplus skin and give a 'cleaner' look to the neck for instance!

Other breeds are shown standing naturally so the judge often has to move round to see the views he wants. Time should be allowed for a naturally shown dog to settle. There is no point in looking at it if it is tugging on the lead or jumping up at its owner.

Judging Dalmatians at Crufts. First the teeth: are they level? Has the dog got a good bite? Is the jaw straight and square?

2   Now the dog should be looked at from the side. The following points should be carefully noted: outline of the head, position and amount of stop where applicable, position, colour and shape of eye, position, size and shape of ears, set of head on neck, length of neck, position and set of neck on body, length of back, line of back, set of tail, length and/or shape of tail, the front legs (particularly the position of the point of elbow in relation to the brisket and the line of the leg in

relation to the withers), the line of brisket and belly, the back legs (particularly the angles of hock and stifle) and, lastly, the shape and position of the feet.

What does the dog look like in outline? Is it well-balanced and is it sound?

How does it move? Is it well put together?

3 The dog should then be looked at from the rear. Now the formation of the legs (hocks or feet turned in or out), the line of the tail and the extent of muscle on the thighs should be observed.

4 The judge should now move round the dog checking markings if applicable.

5 Now from the front. The length, position and shape of ears, position, colour and shape of eyes and the outline of the head and skull should be assessed. The front legs, particularly the position and placement of the elbows (are they tied-in or sticking out), and whether the legs are straight or the feet toeing in or spread out should be noted.

6 Now the overall expression of the dog should be assessed. The judge needs to observe if the impression given is pleasing, alert, intelligent and well-proportioned or dull, coarse and flat?

7 Looking at the dog from the side again the judge now looks at the complete impression the dog makes. Has it got 'style'? Does it look balanced and comfortable and does it give the impression of health and strength? How much does the coat contribute to this impression and is the colour clean and clear?

At this stage the dog has still not been touched and many of the questions posed will still remain if the breed is coated or trimmed. In the physical examination these unanswered questions will have to be kept in mind.

8 It is always best to approach the dog from the front. A hand should be held out, lightly clenched and with palm down for the dog to scent. The age of the dog is often requested at this stage, if appropriate. (In theory, there should never be any necessity to ask the age of a dog. The judge is asked to assess the dog against the standard only so the age of the dog is no more relevant than the age of the handler.)

9 The mouth is then examined with the teeth closed and then the jaws checked. The questions to be asked here are: what is the 'bite' like? Are the jaws 'in line' in both planes? Are the teeth even? Are they all present?

10 At this stage a closer look at the head is required. The judge has to ask himself: how are the features of the head put together? Is any feature too prominent? Are the proportions pleasing? What markings are there on the head? Does this affect the expression at all? (In many breeds the head is the epitomy of type. It is most important that the judge should be able to analyse all the features quickly and accurately.)

11 Moving up to the dog from the side one hand should be placed on the withers to find the highest point of the scapulae. It is important that there is enough space between them just above the spine, particularly in the narrow-chested breeds. If the other hand is now placed on the chest to locate the point of shoulder the first hand can be dropped down to the point of elbow. More questions: is the imaginary line so drawn

vertical and what is the approximate angle made by the two bones? (Some judges like to raise the paw from the ground so that the movement of the scapula and humerus can be clearly seen or felt.) Is the distance between the elbows sufficient or too great – one finger width, two, a span, more? Are the bones of the legs straight? What shape are the feet?

12 Now the rib cage is assessed: how wide is the chest cavity? How does it compare with the distance between the legs at the elbow? Feel the point of elbow: is it beneath the barrel of the chest? Does the brisket start to curve towards the belly before the ribs end? How deep and what shape is the chest cavity?

13 Then the coat is examined: is it a single or double coat? How is the coat coloured? How dense is it? What texture is it?

14 Having located the last rib at the point where it joins the spine there are yet more questions to be asked: does it point forward, down or back? Does it spring out from the spine or is it sharply curved and then flat? What is the distance between the last rib and the pelvis? This is the loin and just below the loin is the area which joins the front assembly to the rear assembly – the 'coupling'.

15 Now the line of the back: does the spine rise or fall and what is the extent of the drop over the pelvis?

16 At this stage the judge will ask himself how much weight the dog is carrying. Too little, too much and, if too much, is it fat or is it muscle?

17 Now the tail: are there any kinks or lumps? Is it held straight or curled and, if curled, what is the extent of the curl?

18 The pelvis: how much does it slope from the horizontal and at what angle does the femur leave the pelvic socket?

19 The back legs: are the joints firm? Are the bones straight and what is the angle between the femur and the tibia in the natural standing position? What is the shape and disposition of the feet?

20 Now the physical examination is complete the judge can stand back and take a last look at the dog: did his physical examination confirm his first impressions? Or did it give him cause for concern?

Eventually this procedure, which sounds very complicated when written out, becomes almost instinctive. However, the judge must allow time at the end of each examination to 'sum up' each dog in his mind. This is most important as there is a tendency to stop thinking about the good points of a given dog once something has been discovered that is 'wrong' with it. This is fault judging and should be avoided. The good and not so good points of each dog should be mentally noted and they should be retained throughout the class. This requires plenty of practice as well as a good memory!

After the physical examination the exhibitor is asked to move the dog. The most usual and convenient pattern (if the ring allows) is to work along the perimeter of an imaginary triangle with the judge standing at one corner. In some small rings it might be necessary to ask the handler to take the dog up and down the ring twice – once with the judge seeing the movement coming and going and once from the side. However, assuming a triangle, the dog is first observed moving away. Handlers should be encouraged to allow the dog to move on a loose lead so the natural gait of the dog can be seen. Answers are required to the following questions. Do the feet pick up smoothly and cleanly? Are the back feet moving in the same plane as the front feet? (If they are not we say that the dog is 'crabbing'.) Does each leg remain straight so that the column of bones is not bent or broken? Does the rump bounce or roll? Do both legs share the work equally? (If they do not, the dog limps!) Does either leg 'throw', hop or hesitate?

As well as assessing conformation and movement, a judge must examine each dog to ensure that it has a typical expression

As the dog moves across the field of vision there is even more to look for. Does the line of the back move parallel to the ground? (The line of the back will quite naturally move up and down but, at the trot, it should retain its natural shape.) Do the withers bounce or pitch? Is the dog pacing? Do the legs off the ground leave the surface at the same time? As the front leg leaves the ground is the back leg behind, beside or in front of it? Is the length of stride the optimum for the breed? Is the head held in the most comfortable and efficient position? Is the dog 'running downhill' or pounding?

As the dog moves towards the judge he should ask himself yet more questions. Do the feet pick up smoothly and cleanly? Are they moving in the same plane as the back feet? Does each leg remain straight so that the column of bones is not bent or broken? Are the elbows tied-in or do they flap out? Do the feet cross or splay?

A judge should not be afraid to move a dog a second or a third time. Uneven ground, a slippery floor and attractive smells, to say nothing of the other dogs in the ring, can all cause a sound dog to move badly. It is important to give each dog a fair chance of getting into his stride. On the other hand, the whole point of a dog show is to see the dogs looking good and a particular animal must be spectacular for a judge to consider placing it without having evidence that it can move properly.

Having seen the dog moving, many judges like to see it standing again. This is a very sound procedure as it helps to integrate what was observed when watching the dog's action with what was discovered during the physical examination. It is also a point at which the dog can be seen standing naturally and, in those breeds which are shown 'stacked', this can be very revealing.

As the seen dog returns to its place, the steward should have the next one ready to come forward.

There is obviously an enormous amount which must be taken into consideration with every dog and I hope that this brief summary shows exactly how much a judge needs to know before they can confidently give an opinion. Now taking into consideration that every breed has different requirements under every heading, the complexity of the task is increased one hundred fold.

After every dog in the class has been seen, decisions need to be made. In many cases there are several dogs which stand out from the rest so the task is easier. In other circumstances the judge must weigh up a dog of good breed type against a dog which is rather plain but moves very well, or decide whether, in a particular instance, a rather straight hock can be forgiven if the dog has other, highly desirable, characteristics.

At most shows five dogs are required to be placed as 1st, 2nd, 3rd, Reserve and Very Highly Commended. They should be 'pulled out' into the centre of the ring and placed, in order, from left to right so that there can be no misunderstanding. When the class has been completed, the steward calls out the numbers and distributes the prize cards. At this stage the judge copies the winning numbers, in order, into the judging book and makes short notes on each of the first three dogs for the report. Some judges use a miniature tape recorder for this and it is certainly quicker.

At the end of the classes (or group of classes if the sexes are judged separately) the unbeaten dogs are called into the ring for the judge to make the Best of Breed or Best of Sex award. This is judged in exactly the same way as a class, although the judge does not usually have to go through the whole procedure. If the sexes are judged separately the two winners are finally brought into the ring for the Best of Breed award. (This procedure, of course, is not followed in Variety classes, although it is followed in the Not Separately Classified classes.)

Throughout judging it is essential that the judge is courteous and polite to all exhibitors. Part of this courtesy is shown in the way a judge dresses. Large hats, dangling jewellery, flapping ties and eccentric accessories are likely to disturb dogs which might otherwise take the class in their stride. And even if the dogs do not notice, the exhibitors certainly will. They are paying for the judge's opinion on the dog, not for a fashion show!

It is also important to ensure that exhibitors and stewards all know what to do and that any requests in the ring are made clearly. Exhibitors are not always polite (neither are some judges), but that is no reason for the judge to lose his temper. Cool, calm and collected should be the key words.

Before judging it is probably not wise to have long and detailed discussions with any of the exhibitors, although this does not mean that anyone should be ignored. Afterwards, exhibitors may wish to discuss particular dogs and particular placings and I believe that the good judge should always be prepared (and able) to do this. Criticism should be accepted politely (unless the judge is very sure of his grounds) but anything said by exhibitors about their own or other people's dogs should be checked with experts before it is accepted!

REPORTS

Most exhibitors expect their judge to write a report. Reading most of those printed in the canine press I often wonder what the point of this is; most are cliché-ridden and predictable. But just occasionally they can describe and illuminate a dog in a way that makes it all worthwhile.

Report writing is a skill that needs practice just as much as judging. It needs a lot of thought, too, for a report can damn a dog for its whole career if it draws attention to a fault which might only be temporary (monorchidism in a youngster, for instance) or if it is simply inaccurate because the judge does not really know the breed.

Personally, I like reports to be positive and, to be honest, most exhibitors prefer it that way! I believe that the best answer is a short summary, prior to the individual reports of the dogs, which specifies any general concerns the judge has about the breed. This gives the best of both worlds and if exhibitors are worried about the points made, they can approach the judge later and request more detail.

Myths and Legends

I wrote earlier in this chapter that any prospective judge did not only need a great deal of background knowledge of dogs in general as well as detailed and specific knowledge of each breed, but that there were a number of books that should be required reading. However, because the business of dog judging and of canine movement has not really been thoroughly researched many books do not always give accurate information. There are four particular areas which need clarification. These are angulation, drive, balance and single-tracking.

ANGULATION

Briefly, this is a term used to describe the angles between adjacent bones in the fore- and hindquarters. Two statements are often made which are inaccurate. The first is that good movement is impossible unless the angles between scapula and humerus in the forehand and the pelvis and femur in the hindquarters are equal when the dog is standing naturally. This is not true. Any slow-motion film of a Greyhound running will show that the angle between scapula and humerus is much greater than between the pelvis and femur – and Greyhounds are probably the most efficient as well as the fastest movers in the canine world. This is not to say that these angles are not often equal, but it is misleading, to say the least, to imply that it is a necessity.

The second is that the 'ideal' angle between scapula and humerus is 90 degrees. Take a large protractor to any breed of dog and I guarantee that you will not find one which, relaxed and standing naturally, has an angle between these two bones of less than 100 degrees, and most are more like 115–120 degrees. Certainly a 60-degree slope of shoulder (that is the angle of the spine of the scapula measured to a horizontal line) is not at all unusual. Whether you are judging Whippets or Weimaraners, if you are taking accepted good angulation as one of your criteria, then you would, of necessity, reject them all!

DRIVE

Many standards and most breeders and judges often use the phrase 'drives well from behind'. If you ask any of these groups to apportion the amount of power between the forequarter and the hindquarters in percentage terms the answer is usually 30 per cent from the front and 70 per cent from the rear. This dictum has been accepted as gospel for years – but it is not true. Tests at Bristol University during the mid-1970s showed that the *average* drive at varying speeds and gaits and using varying breeds was 48 per cent from the front and 52 per cent from the rear. The details of the research, which cover several printed pages, are too complex to go into here, but it just goes to show how easy it is to pick up inaccurate information.

BALANCE

A number of books attempt to analyse canine movement in engineering terms. This is fine if you are an engineer, but if you are not it is easy to come unstuck. One particular theory which has been published over and over again implies that because the dog has support at four points it has four 'centres of gravity'. This really is nonsense. It means 'points of support', but even substituting the correct definition does not really improve the thesis. What these ideas are really trying to say is that whenever a dog's limbs are *carrying weight* (whether they be standing still or moving) there should be a 'single column of support' from the ground to the point at which the limb joins the body. What the limbs are doing at other times is not really important (although, aesthetically, it is more acceptable if they move efficiently and smoothly).

SINGLE-TRACKING

This concept is closely allied to the question of balance. When dogs begin to move their pads move forward either side of a central line. As speed increases, there is a *tendency* for the pads to be set down closer to that central line. In many breeds the pads quickly tread the centre line and this is known as single-tracking. Not all breeds actually single track (the Welsh Corgi and the Bulldog do not have a conformation which allows it) but all of them show the *tendency* to do so.

ABOUT 'TYPE'

Despite not wanting to get involved with too much theory, a brief word about type is essential in a book of this nature. People often find the concept difficult to understand but I hope the following will be helpful.

Imagine a well-known building – St Paul's Cathedral will do nicely. There are many ways in which an artist can interpret St Paul's to others: he could use a camera and a whole range of photographic techniques; he could draw it with a pen, a pencil, or a brush; in watercolours, mediums or oils; he could make a model or an etching, a lithograph or a print. Whatever method he used the building would still be immediately recognizable as St Paul's. These different techniques may be compared to the various breeds of dog. The essential elements are the same but the appearance, size and proportions are different.

Let us now look at one of the techniques. If a dozen artists are asked to paint St Paul's in oil paints, each will interpret the building in a different way. Even if we asked them to paint as accurate a picture as the possibly could, we should easily be able to distinguish between the work of one artist and another. These differences can be compared to the different strains within any given breed and are the reasons why the stock from one kennel is often quite clearly different from that of another.

If we now take all these oil paintings and put them in front of a group of art experts (or even well-informed non-experts) they would be able to clearly distinguish between the work that was good, bad or indifferent. They might not all agree on which painting was the 'best' and which was 'second best' and so on, but the best artists would certainly stand out from the rest. The building has remained the same throughout the exercise but Man's interpretation was developed in varying ways. I hope that the analogy has proved helpful even if it is, perhaps, oversimplified.

Summing Up

A judge holds an extremely responsible position within the world of dogs. The results of one show or the award of one Challenge Certificate are relatively unimportant but, in the long term, judges do have an effect on a breed and they should be aware that their decisions are of considerable importance.

Judging is not the simple process of choosing the dog you like best – anyone can do that – or even, as some would say, choosing the dog in a class you would select for breeding. Naturally, no judge worth his salt would put up a dog which he would not be prepared to breed from but, in the show ring, style, temperament and showmanship as well as the requirements of the standard must always be borne in mind.

The key concepts are experience, talent, knowledge, integrity and decisiveness. Becoming accepted as a judge is a long-term business, too, so considerable tenacity is also required. Anyone lacking in any of these qualities is unlikely to make a good judge.

5 Records

The usefulness and necessity of accurate records are almost impossible to estimate for they not only provide the information required for the day-to-day running of the world of dogs but, in the long term, provide the basis upon which the quality of the dogs being bred can be built. In this chapter I intend to summarize these records which are of the greatest importance to each of the activities involved in the exhibition of show dogs in the United Kingdom.

Some records are centralized by the Kennel Club and these are:

DOGS

1   The registration of all dogs that are shown or bred from and whose progeny are shown in this country or exported for showing or breeding abroad.
2   The ownership of every registered dog.
3   The affix of every recognized breeder in the United Kingdom.
4   The basic breeding records of each dog and bitch used.
5   The recorded wins in classes applicable to the Stud Book.
6   Cumulative wins resulting in Champion and Junior Warrant awards.
7   Details of BVA/KC schemes to improve breeding stock when there are hereditary problems within the breed.

CLUBS

1   A copy of the audited balance sheet of every registered canine society.
2   Names and addresses of the officers of every registered canine society.

SHOWS

1   Copies of marked catalogues of every licensed show held in the United Kingdom. (This also gives information about the experience of judges and enables questionnaires to be checked.)
2   Records of judges passed to award tickets and their past and committed appointments.
3   Dates and distribution of shows for the allocation of dates to canine societies.

KENNEL CLUB

1   Lists of members and associates.
2   Records of committee and sub-committee meetings.
3   Accounts.

All the above material is collated and in most instances appears some-where in: the Kennel Club Year Book (each year); the *Kennel Gazette* (each month); the Stud Book (each year); the *Breed Records Supplement* (each month).

Serious breeders, exhibitors, judges and show managements will certainly need to have each of these publications. In fact, members of the Kennel Club, associates and secretaries of canine societies all receive them automatically. Clubs, of course, have a duty to keep them as part of their records and either make them available to their members or publish the relevant sections in their club magazines.

Canine Societies

All canine societies must, of course, keep full records of all their tran-sactions, up-to-date lists of members, minutes of meetings and balance sheets. There are annual returns which must be made to the Kennel Club and members are entitled to know the way in which their associa-tion is being run and how their money is being spent. When there is a change of secretary, it is essential that all records are updated and passed over in a form that is easily comprehensible. A proportion of canine societies are often far too lax about quite simple and essential records and this can cause tremendous problems for the incoming secretary or committee.

Most canine societies own a number of cups and some of these are immensely valuable. The job of the cup steward, therefore, carries very great responsibility and it is most important that a complete list of cups is kept and that signatures on appropriate forms are obtained when they are presented. The cups should be officially valued at least once every ten years and, of course, they should be insured.

Many societies have cups that are awarded as the result of a points system which runs throughout the year (such as Stud Dog or Brood Bitch trophies), so the cup steward, too, should have full details of wins so that claims can be checked.

All clubs should have some form of Third Party Limited Liability insurance. It is cheap because disasters seldom occur but, when they do, few societies would be able to afford a claim.

Breed clubs have a special and extra responsibility. To comply with the rules of their association they need to produce quite full records of the breed which will supplement the rather sketchy and basic facts collected and published by the Kennel Club. They also have the responsibility of ensuring that new owners are given helpful and accurate information about the breed. Most breed clubs produce some sort of regular publication such as a yearbook or magazine. Personally, I should like to see every club have an archivist, too, whose special responsibility it would be to collect any material about the breed that becomes available, to collate it, keep it and regularly publish a bibliography/catalogue. This would be extremely useful for members and for others who are researching the breed.

In breeds where there are recognized hereditary defects, they also have a duty to persuade members to take part in the appropriate scheme as well as keep the necessary records.

The breed clubs are also responsible for compiling judging lists and, in consequence, have the added task of ensuring that both specialist and all-round aspiring judges are provided with both information and, where appropriate, training. Some breed societies even keep records of which judges have officiated and when, and this can be very useful information for championship show administrators when selecting their judges.

The Individual

EXHIBITORS

All exhibitors should have a log book for each dog, showing wins and the level of show. This is valuable for prospective breeders and judges as well as being a worthwhile record over the years. Exhibitors should also ensure that they have a fully marked-up diary, particularly noting the dates of closing of entries. Marked catalogues for every championship show attended and for open shows, too, if the breed is relatively small and the number of Challenge Certificates on offer is therefore on the low side. It is amazing how many arguments can be quickly settled by referring to the appropriate catalogue!

BREEDERS

This is a chapter on its own. Essential records include charts showing all matings and their results, broken down into number of puppies, their sexes, their development and their adult career as pets or as exhibits or breeding stock. Photographs of sires, dams and their progeny as adults are extremely important, as are pictures of stud dogs (and their progeny mated to other bitches) which might be used in the future. Breeding good dogs is a long and difficult task and effective and accurate records can make it a good deal easier.

A diary of each whelping with all the relevant times is also very helpful. This can be referred to on future occasions as, although the first litter bred is often very memorable, after some time it can be difficult to remember precisely what was done under particular circumstances. A diary helps a lot, not only in establishing a recognized pattern within breeding stock but in doing so for individual bitches.

JUDGES

Marked catalogues and a good diary are absolutely essential. As a judge gains experience he will be asked to write down the numbers of dogs and the classes judged at shows going back to the beginning of his career. Accuracy is essential for the Kennel Club has treated cases of 'exaggeration' very, very seriously. I keep a running total of classes judged under Breeds, Not Separately Classified and Varieties and this can simply be photocopied as required.

Every individual should also have a carefully selected library of standard works which, I know, will prove invaluable. My own selection of recommended books is included in the Bibliography – those starred I consider essential to the serious exhibitor, breeder and judge.

Finally, the most prolific record is provided by the canine press (currently *Our Dogs, Dog World* and *Dogs Monthly*). To be frank, much of the material has little more then passing value, although they do regularly print articles of particular interest which are worth saving. Many breeders and exhibitors keep the reports relating to their own dogs or own breed and these can be interesting. However, by its very nature, much of what is printed is quickly out-of-date and there is just as much of a tendency for the press to sensationalize and over-react in an attempt to increase sales in the world of dogs as there is in Fleet Street.

This is not to say that the press do not perform an invaluable function. Their primary responsibility is to provide enthusiasts with up-to-date information on every aspect of the show scene and this they do with commendable accuracy. They also provide a useful forum for the dissemination of ideas as well as being the primary method by which specialist companies can bring their products to the attention of the purchaser. In general I believe that the press serves us well and there can be few regular exhibitors, officials and judges who do not take at least one of the weekly papers and read it very thoroughly.

Appendix:
List of Recognized Breeds

Breed Statistics

TOTAL REGISTRATIONS FOR 1981

SPORTING BREEDS	*1981 Registrations*	*% of total Registrations*
HOUND GROUP		
Afghan Hounds	1187	.69
Basenjis	67	.04
Basset Hounds	713	.41
Beagles	1134	.66
Bloodhounds	90	.05
Borzois	206	.12
Dachshunds (Long-Haired)	490	.28
Dachshunds (Miniature Long-Haired)	1837	1.09
Dachshunds (Smooth-Haired)	444	.26
Dachshunds (Miniature Smooth-Haired)	1010	.59
Dachshunds (Wire-Haired)	284	.16
Dachshunds (Miniature Wire-Haired)	602	.35
Deerhounds	161	.09
Elkhounds	151	.09
Finnish Spitz	55	.03
Greyhounds	57	.03
Ibizan Hounds	15	.01
Irish Wolfhounds	623	.36
Otterhounds	52	.03
Petits Bassets Griffons Vendeen	59	.03
Pharaoh Hounds	36	.02
Rhodesian Ridgebacks	366	.21
Salukis	272	.16
Sloughis	20	.01
Whippets	1417	.82
	11348	

SPORTING BREEDS	1981 Registrations	% of total Registrations
GUNDOG GROUP		
English Setters	1246	.72
German Short-Haired Pointers	850	.49
German Wire-Haired Pointers	84	.05
Gordon Setters	529	.31
Hungarian Vizslas	153	.09
Irish Red and White Setters	49	.03
Irish Setters	3122	1.81
Large Munsterlanders	135	.08
Pointers	838	.49
Retrievers (Chesapeake Bay)	17	.01
Retrievers (Curly Coated)	90	.05
Retrievers (Flat Coated)	667	.35
Retrievers (Golden)	8837	5.13
Retrievers (Labrador)	12543	7.28
Small Munsterlanders	1	.00
ʻSpaniels (American Cocker)	459	.27
Spaniels (American Water)	12	.01
Spaniels (Clumber)	57	.03
Spaniels (Cocker)	8009	4.65
Spaniels (English Springer)	7055	4.09
Spaniels (Field)	79	.05
Spaniels (Irish Water)	98	.06
Spaniels (Sussex)	55	.03
Spaniels (Welsh Springer)	596	.35
Weimaraners	671	.39
	13663	
TERRIER GROUP		
Airedale Terriers	1383	.80
Australian Terriers	83	.05
Bedlington Terriers	200	.12
Border Terriers	1152	.67
Bull Terriers	1426	.83
Bull Terriers (Miniature)	65	.03
Cairn Terriers	2571	1.49
Dandie Dinmont Terriers	204	.12
Fox Terriers (Smooth)	316	.18
Fox Terriers (Wire)	738	.43
Glen of Imaal Terriers	26	.02
Irish Terriers	139	.08
Kerry Blue Terriers	260	.15

SPORTING BREEDS	1981 Registrations	% of total Registrations
TERRIER GROUP—*contd.*		
Lakeland Terriers	273	.16
Manchester Terriers	91	.05
Norfolk Terriers	272	.16
Norwich Terriers	117	.07
Scottish Terriers	904	.52
Sealyham Terriers	140	.08
Skye Terriers	163	.09
Soft-Coated Wheaten Terriers	104	.06
Staffordshire Bull Terriers	3374	1.96
Welsh Terriers	272	.16
West Highland White Terriers	3525	2.05
	17798	
TOTAL SPORTING BREEDS	**75398**	

NON-SPORTING BREEDS	1981 Registrations	% of total Registrations
UTILITY GROUP		
Boston Terriers	93	.03
Bulldogs	805	.47
Chow Chows	1155	.67
Dalmatians	745	.43
French Bulldogs	141	.08
Giant Schnauzers	89	.05
Japanese Akitas	1	.00
Japanese Spitz	41	.02
Keeshonds	198	.11
Leonbergers	1	.00
Lhasa Apsos	965	.56
Miniature Schnauzers	751	.44
Poodles (Miniature)	1781	1.03
Poodles (Standard)	794	.46
Poodles (Toy)	3567	2.07
Schipperkes	76	.04
Schnauzers	98	.06
Shih Tzus	1528	.89
Tibetan Spaniels	430	.25
Tibetan Terriers	404	.23
	13663	

NON-SPORTING BREEDS	1981 Registrations	% of total Registrations
WORKING GROUP		
Alaskan Malamutes	15	.01
Anatolian (Karabash) Dogs	31	.02
Australian Cattle Dogs	14	.01
Australian Kelpies	5	.00
Bearded Collies	1179	.68
Belgian Shepherd Dogs (Groenendaels)	149	.09
Belgian Shepherd Dogs (Malinois)	17	.01
Belgian Shepherd Dogs (Tervuerens)	109	.06
Bernese Mountain Dogs	199	.12
Border Collies	718	.42
Bouviers Des Flandres	56	.03
Boxers	3947	2.29
Briards	176	.10
Bullmastiffs	422	.22
Collies (Rough)	6059	3.52
Collies (Smooth)	49	.03
Dobermanns	4824	2.80
Estrela Mountain Dogs	17	.01
German Shepherd Dogs (Alsatians)	16068	9.32
Great Danes	2381	1.38
Hovawarts	6	.01
Hungarian Pulis	64	.04
Lancashire Heelers	3	.00
Komondors	9	.01
Maremma Sheepdogs	77	.04
Mastiffs	241	.14
Neapolitan Mastiffs	1	.00
Newfoundlands	349	.20
Norwegian Buhunds	81	.05
Old English Sheepdogs	3940	2.29
Pinschers	1	.00
Portuguese Water Dogs	5	.01
Pyrenean Mountain Dogs	430	.25
Rottweilers	1641	.95
St Bernards	559	.32
Samoyeds	749	.43
Shetland Sheepdogs	4198	2.44
Siberian Huskies	52	.03
Swedish Vallhunds	42	.02
Tibetan Mastiffs	2	.00
Welsh Corgis (Cardigan)	132	.08
Welsh Corgis (Pembroke)	1475	.86
	50492	

NON-SPORTING BREEDS	1981 Registrations	% of total Registrations
TOY GROUP		
Affenpinschers	25	.01
Australian Silky Terriers	24	.01
Bichons Frises	387	.22
Cavalier King Charles Spaniels	8530	4.95
Chihuahuas (Long-Coat)	1938	1.12
Chihuahuas (Smooth-Coat)	1071	.59
Chinese Crested Dogs	75	.04
English Toy Terriers (Black and Tan)	50	.03
Griffons Bruxellois	247	.14
Italian Greyhounds	133	.08
Japanese Chins	166	.10
King Charles Spaniels	205	.12
Lowchens	94	.05
Maltese	436	.25
Miniature Pinschers	181	.11
Papillons	755	.44
Pekingese	2650	1.54
Pomeranians	1057	.61
Pugs	632	.37
Yorkshire Terriers	14149	8.21
	32805	
TOTAL NON-SPORTING BREEDS	**96960**	
TOTAL SPORTING BREEDS	75398	
Total Registrations for the Year	**172358**	

Reproduced with the permission of the Kennel Club

Glossary

ACHILLES TENDON — The large tendon extending to the os calsis and formed by uniting small tendons of the lower thigh; muscles pulling on the achilles tendon straighten the hock.

ALBINO — An animal born with deficiency of pigments in the skin, eyes and hair; eyes, nose and eye rims are pink. Hair is always white.

ALMOND EYES — Eyes that appear shaped like almonds. The eyeball, of course, is round; it is the surrounding tissue that creates the almond shape.

ANGULATION — The angle formed between leg bones (including shoulder blades and pelvis), particularly applicable to the stifle, hock and shoulder angulation.

APPLE HEAD — Roundness of topskull; like an apple. A Chihuahua has a well-rounded 'apple dome' skull, but several breeds call an apple head a fault.

ARCHED — Applied to the neck, back or toes when arched; rounded upwards. The arch may be formed by muscles or bones. Arched loin (caused by muscles); arched toes (caused by bones); arched back (camel back).

BACK — The anatomical division of the spine is neck, withers, back, loin and croup, each variable in meaning depending upon the context of the Standard. In a few dog Standards, the five vertebrae between the withers and loin.

BALANCED — *See* Symmetry.

BELTON — A coat colour, especially of English Setters. A coat with ticking or flecking in the base colour (white): blue belton (dilute black or black ticking); orange belton; liver belton; or lemon belton. Ticking is a genetic pattern that may carry any pigment as black, tan (brown) or yellow.

BITCHY — Effeminate male (derogatory) or typically feminine female.

BITE — Determined when the mouth is closed. The position of the upper and lower teeth relative to one another. Level bite is where the upper and lower teeth meet exactly. In a scissors bite the upper teeth extend beyond the lower teeth, but surfaces touch one another. *See also* overshot and undershot.

BLAZE — A white stripe or line extending up the centre of the face.

BLOCKY — Applied to the head or body; square or cube-like.

BLOOM — A coat in prime condition 'blooms'; the sheen, glossiness of the coat.

BLUE MERLE — *See* Merle.

BOBTAIL — Dog with tail bobbed (docked or natural). Also the nickname of the Old English Sheepdog.

BONE — Used to mean substance as in 'plenty of bone' or 'well-boned'; size (diameter) of bone; reverse of light-boned.

BRACE — Two dogs shown as a matched pair.

BREED — A type of dog developed by man and requiring control by man to prevent intermixing of breeds; dogs that more or less produce like themselves.

BRINDLE — A coat colour consisting of a mixture of black lines and a lighter colour arranged into a striped pattern.

BRISKET — Lower part of the chest between and in front of the legs; deep brisket or shallow brisket indicates the depth of chest.

BROKEN COLOUR — A solid colour broken by white (sometimes other colours).

BULL NECK — A heavy neck; well-muscled neck, often short.

BUTTERFLY NOSE — A nose with flesh-coloured spots; usually undesirable or faulty.

BUTTON EAR — Top of ear folded forwards so as to close the ear-opening with the tip near the skull; ear is pointed towards the eyes.

CAMEL BACK	Arched back like that of a one-humped camel. Usually a fault.
CANINE	Dog family (dogs, wolves, jackals and foxes).
CANINES	Fang-like teeth behind incisors.
CARPALS	Bones of the pastern joints.
CARTILAGE	A somewhat elastic tissue that often serves as bones in embryo; it forms a bearing surface in joints; gristle.
CASTRATION	The removal of testicals by surgery.
CAT-FOOT	A paw resembling a cat's foot (not including claws); foot is round and compact.
CENTRE OF GRAVITY	A point in the body at which the entire weight can be considered as concentrated; the centre of gravitational attraction; an imaginary point used in engineering calculations where the entire weight of a body can be considered as concentrated.
CHALLENGE CERTIFICATE	Certificate award by a judge to Best of Sex at a championship show. *See also* Champion.
CHAMPION	A title bestowed upon a dog that has been awarded three Challenge Certificates under three different judges.
CHEEKY	Cheeks prominently rounded. Well-developed cheek muscles in retrievers are undesirable (retrievers should be soft-mouthed and well-developed jaw muscles prevent the gentle pick-up of birds).
CHEST	The part of the body enclosed by ribs and breastbone.
CHINA EYE	A clear blue eye.
CHINESE-EYED	Outside corner of eyes higher than the inner corner.
CHIPPENDALE FRONT	Front shaped like a Chippendale chair.
CHISELLED	Cut-away or clean-cut. Usually used in description of head shape.
CHOPS	A jaw; commonly the fleshy parts about the jaw as in the Bulldog Standard.
CLIPPING	The back foot striking the front foot in a dog's gait; trimming a coat.
CLODDY	Of low stature and heavy; usually a fault.
CLOSE-COUPLED	Short between the last rib and the thigh.
COARSE	Unrefined.
COAT	Hairy covering on a dog.
COBBY	Compact.

COLLAR	A coat colour marking around the neck; a white collar; also a leather collar around the neck for leading a dog.
COLOUR, COAT	Hairs contain rings of pigments in these colours: black, brown (tan) or yellow (white has no colour pigments). All coat colours and patterns are varying arrangements of pigment rings.
CONDITION	Health as shown by flesh, coat sheen, eyes, reflexes and behaviour.
CONFORMATION	The sum of the parts of a dog – the way it is 'put together'. Also conformation with the Standard; agreement of the dog with the written Standard.
COUPLING	The loin; the flesh area between the ribs and the pelvis.
COVERING GROUND	The ratio of the distance between the ground and brisket and the distance between front and rear legs.
COW-HOCKED	Hocks similar to those of most cows, ie hocks turned inwards, toward one another; fault in most dogs.
CRABBING	The act of a dog moving with its back at an angle with its direction of travel; a fault in most dogs.
CROPPING	Surgically removing the outer part of ears to make them stand erect. In the UK cropping is illegal and dogs with cropped ears may not be shown. However, it is common in the USA and on the Continent.
CROSSING OVER	Legs crossing one another; better known as weaving; a leg swinging in an arc around the support leg is said to cross over.
CROUP	The portion of the body above the hind legs and extending from the loin to the tail. The pelvis is a part of the croup.
CRYPTORCHID	A condition of the adult male when the testicles have not descended into the scrotum.
CULOTTE	Long hair on back of thighs.
CUSHION	Padding to the upper lip.
DAPPLED	Variegated with spots or patches of a different shade; marked with small spots; usually by a merling gene.
DEWCLAW	Unused digit (toe) on the inside of the leg.

Dewclaws are usually removed at birth. In a few breeds (Pyrenean Mountain Dog and Briard) they must be present.

DEWLAP — Loose pendulous skin under the throat, as on a Bloodhound. A dog that is not supposed to have dewlap and does is said to be throaty.

DIAPHRAGM — The muscular tissue separating the thorax and the abdomen; the breathing diaphragm.

DIGITS — Bones of the toes (first three bones of each toe).

DISH-FACED — The nose curves like a dish; the top line of the muzzle is concave.

DISQUALIFICATION — A fault that renders a dog ineligible to compete at a show.

DISTEMPER TEETH — Pitting of the tooth enamel; often caused by distemper or other illness occurring at time of teething.

DOCK — To surgically remove tail or portion of the tail; a docked tail.

DOMED — Domed skull; rounded in topskull; not flat; convex.

DOUBLE COAT — Two coats; a soft undercoat for warmth and waterproofing, along with a hard outer-coat resistant to wear.

DOWN-FACE — Muzzle inclining downwards as on a Bull Terrier; the topline of an egg-shaped muzzle; a fault on many breeds.

DRAUGHT DOGS — Dogs designed to pull sledges or carts.

DROP EAR — Not erect or prick; ends of ear dropping or folding forwards.

DUDLEY NOSE — Flesh-coloured nose. Usually eye rims are the same colour.

ELBOW — The joint between the upper arm and the forearm (humerus and radius).

ELBOWS OUT — Out at elbows; elbows not too close to body; upper arm and lower arm projecting out from the body.

EWE NECK — Neck concave; like the neck of a sheep; not an arched neck.

EYES — The shape of the surrounding tissues determines the apparent eye shape as called for in Standards. The eyeball is invariably round.

EYE TEETH — Upper canines.

FALL — Hair falling over face.

FANGS	Canine teeth.
FEATHERING	Long hair on back of legs or underside of tail.
FEET, EAST AND WEST	Toes turned out.
FEMUR	Bone below pelvis; upper thigh bone; bone between pelvis and stifle joint.
FIBULA	Smaller of two bones between stifle and hock joints; located in lower thigh.
FLAG	Tail with long hair; a feathered tail as on an Irish Setter.
FLANK	Area between last rib and thigh; the area thinly covered with flesh and skin between the last rib and hindquarters.
FLASHY	Superficial traits that attract favourable attention.
FLAT BONE	Leg bone elliptical; not rounded or, put simply, 'straight'.
FLEWS	Pendulous upper lip, especially in the corners.
FLOATING RIB	The last or thirteenth rib which is not attached to other ribs.
FLYING EARS	Ears that show excessive erectile power are said to 'fly'. A dog with semi-prick ears which stand up has 'flying ears'. Ears pricked up more than is correct for the breed.
FOREARM	The portion of the leg between the elbow and pastern.
FORECHEST	The part of the dog in front of the points of the shoulder blades.
FOREFACE	All of the portion of the head in front of the eyes.
FOREHAND	Forequarters; all of the front leg including shoulder blade.
FOXY	Expression of face that looks like a fox; pointed nose with short foreface; a sharp face.
FRINGES	Feathering.
FRONT	Front legs, chest, brisket and withers, but not head.
FRONTAL BONE	The skull bones over the eyes.
FURROW	Median line (caused by indentation) of skull.
GAIT	Manner in which a dog moves, as walking, trotting, pacing or galloping.
GALLOP	A fast, running gait; canter, normal gallop or the double suspension gallop.
GUARD HAIRS	The longer hairs on double-coated dogs; stiffer hairs that protect the undercoat.

GAY TAIL	A tail carried higher than desirable for the breed; usually the tail is held over the back.
GAZEHOUND	Hounds that hunt game by sight, such as Greyhounds, Whippets, Saluki, Borzoi or Afghan Hounds.
GOOSE-RUMP	Croup (pelvis) sloping too steeply toward the rear; low-tail set.
GROUP	Dog breeds are divided into six groups to facilitate judging.
HACKLES	Raise hackles; in anger a dog that involuntarily raises the hair on his neck and top of back is said to have his hackles up.
HACKNEY ACTION	High lifting of the front leg with pastern and paw pointed downward; named after the hackney horse; approved in Miniature Pinscher Standard.
HARD-MOUTHED	Retrievers should be soft-mouthed; a dog that leaves tooth marks on retrieved game is said to be hard-mouthed.
HAREFOOT	Foot as on a hare or rabbit; an elongated foot; a narrow long foot.
HARLEQUIN	A coat colour, patched or pied; Great Danes with black patches on white.
HAW	A membrane in the inside corner of the eye (a third eyelid). Bassets, Bloodhounds and Otterhounds should show haws; most other breeds consider showing the haw as a fault.
HEAT	Oestrus; breeding period of bitches.
HEIGHT	Height as measured from tip of shoulder blade to floor; height at withers.
HERRING GUT	Bottom line of dog sweeps up from brisket to loin; ribs rapidly slope upward from keel to floating rib; a fault that decreases heart room.
HINDQUARTERS	Rear assembly of dog (pelvis, thighs, hocks and paws).
HIP JOINT	Ball and socket joint attaching rear leg at pelvis.
HOCK	The hock joint, lower joint on rear leg; often incorrectly used to mean the area from the hock joint to the paw.
HOCKS WELL LET DOWN	Hock joints close to the ground. 'Short' hocks improve endurance. 'Long' hocks improve speed.
HONOURABLE SCARS	Scars resulting from injuries acquired when

	doing useful work, as hunting scars.
HUMERUS	Bone between elbow and shoulder blade; upper arm bone.
INCISORS	Front teeth between canines; six front teeth in each jaw between the fangs (canines).
JAWS	The jaw bones carry the teeth; upper and lower jaws border the mouth.
JOWLS	Lips and flesh of the jaw.
JUDGE	At a dog show, one appointed to classify dogs in order of merit; one who gives a judgment on dogs.
KINETIC BALANCE	Balance when in motion; a bicycle and rider is in balance when in motion (the rider falls off when not in balance).
KNEE	The stifle joint (not pastern joint on front leg).
KNEE JOINT	Stifle joint in rear leg.
KNUCKLING OVER	Pastern joint bent forward; instead of being vertical the front leg has a forward bend at the pastern joint.
LATERAL DISPLACEMENT	Lateral instability; the force that causes side sway in a pacing dog (to a lesser degree in the trotting dog).
LAYBACK	There are two distinct meanings of 'layback'. The first and most common is to describe 'shoulder slope' of the scapula from the point of shoulder to the withers. Some prefer to always refer to this as the 'slope of shoulder' and reserve 'layback' for convergence of the scapulae over the ribs towards the withers, ie the slope as seen from the front of the dog rather than the side.
LEATHER	The leather of a hound's ear; the soft portion of an ear; the flap of an ear.
LEGGY	Legs too long for the dog.
LEVEL BACK	Back level (loin may be arched and the back level if the Standard of the breed describes the 'back' as being that portion of the spine to which the ribs are attached).
LEVEL BITE	*See* Bite.
LEVEL GAIT	The dog moves without rise or fall of the withers; a good German Shepherd trot.
LIPPY	Lips that do not fit tightly or which are thick and full.
LIVER	A coat colour of deep reddish brown often

associated with yellow eyes.

LOADED SHOULDERS	Over-development of muscles loaded under the shoulder blade (causes the dog to be out at the elbow).
LOIN	Area between the last rib and thigh; area thinly covered with skin and muscle between floating rib and croup.
LOOSE SHOULDERS	Shoulder muscles not tight; the dog may paddle because of loose shoulders.
LOWER THIGH	Lower portion of thigh; second thigh; from the stifle to the hock.
MASK	Dark shading on the muzzle.
MEDIAN LINE	Indentation causing line in the skull extending from stop to occiput.
MERLE	A pattern of coat colouration; mottled blue colour pattern found in Collies and Shetland Sheepdogs; sometimes with flecks of black; merle is a pattern and the colour is specified as for example, blue merle.
METACARPUS	Bones of front leg from pastern joint to foot.
METATARSUS	Bones of rear leg from hock joint to foot.
MILK TEETH	Baby teeth; first teeth.
MOLARS	The dog has four premolars on each side of the upper and lower jaw. There are two true molars on each side of the upper jaw and three on each side of the lower jaw.
MOLERA	Incomplete closing of bones in skull (Chihuahua).
MONORCHID	A male dog with one testicle in the scrotum (there may be one in the abdominal cavity).
MUZZLE	The protruding jaw and nose; the head in front of the eyes. Also a device fitting over a dog's mouth to prevent biting or eating.
NECK	The area between the head and the shoulders; included are the first seven vertebrae of the spinal column.
OCCIPUT	(Pronounced Ox-i-put) Back part of the head or skull; the high point of the back part of the head.
OCCIPITAL PROTUBERANCE	Some hounds and gun dogs have the occiput well-developed; the occipital protuberance.
ORANGE BELTON	*See* Belton.
OS CALCIS	The larger bone of the hock joint; the achilles tendon pulling on this bone gives action to the

	leg below the hock joint.
OTTER TAIL	Tapering tail, thick and flat at the root and with hair parted on the underside.
OUT AT SHOULDERS	Points of shoulder blade too far apart at the withers for a given breed.
OVAL CHEST	Chest deeper than wide.
OVERSHOT	The upper jaw overshooting the lower jaw (overshot and undershot are relative to the lower jaw); pig jaw; upper jaw extending beyond lower jaw; a fault in all breeds.
PACE	A gait; two right feet on the ground and two left feet in the air followed by two left feet on the ground and two right feet in the air; in some breeds the 'pace' is acceptable.
PADDING	Flapping; the front feet flap up (opposite of hackney action where the toe points downward); more common in short-legged breeds, such as Dachshunds. Also hitting the pad on the ground prior to the normal full forward swing of the front leg.
PADDLING	Moving the front legs like a canoe paddle motion; a rotary motion; when the front feet move forward they have a somewhat circular motion.
PADS	Tough soft material on underside of dog's feet; pads absorb shock.
PARTI-COLOUR	A coat with patches of two or more colours; three colours are usually designated as tri-coloured.
PASTERN	The region between the wrist and toes on forelegs; pastern joint is at the wrist (carpus); down in pasterns is an excessive forward sloping pastern for the breed; knuckled-over occurs when pastern joint bends forwards and the pastern slopes backwards.
PATELLA	Kneecap.
PEAR-SHAPED	Shaped like a pear; body of a Bulldog is pear-shaped.
PELVIS	Bone fused to spinal column at rear of dog; used to support hind legs.
PENCILING	In Manchester Terriers the black line dividing the tan on the toes.
PENDULOUS	Long and hanging as pendulous ears; like the pendulum (hanging); usually wide at bottom.

PIED	Piebald; parti-coloured; large patches of two or more colours.
PIGEON-BREASTED	A short protruding breastbone.
PIGEON-TOED	Toes turned in; toes pointing towards one another; toes turned in from the line of progress.
PIG JAW	*See* Overshot.
PIGMENTATION	Dark pigmentation of nose and eyelids; 'lacking pigment' indicates light colour.
PINCER BITE	Level bite; upper and lower incisors (front teeth) meet level; not a scissors bite.
PLUME	Hair on tail as on Setters; a long fringe of hair hanging from tail; also applied to Pomeranian and Pekingese tails; a heavy coated tail carried over back.
POMPOM	Pertains to Poodles; a round tuft of hair on the end of the tail produced by trimming.
POUNDING	Feet (front) hitting the ground too hard.
PRICK EAR	An erect ear; usually pointed and erect.
PROFESSIONAL HANDLER	A dog handler who shows other people's dogs for a fee.
PUPPY	At dog shows, a dog under one year of age. In the UK dogs may not be shown if they are under six months old.
PUT DOWN	A dog put down (prepared) for the show ring, usually by trimming, combing, grooming and beautifying. A slang expression describing an unplaced dog; a dog is put down when it does not win a competition.
QUALITY	A dog has quality; a refinement of appearance for the breed; not coarse.
QUARTERS	Usually used as hindquarters or forequarters.
RACY	Tall and thin as a Greyhound; too light in structure.
REACH	The distance the front or rear legs can reach (forward reach or back reach).
RETRIEVE	The act of bringing back game (or dumbell in obedience ring) to handler; bringing back an object.
RIBBED-UP	Well ribbed-up; long ribs that angle back from the spinal column (45 degrees is ideal) and the last rib is long (the loin is short).
RIBS WELL-SPRUNG	Ribs spring out from the back nearly level and form an angle with the spinal column (a 45

degrees angle between spinal column and rib is best). Well-sprung refers more to the way the ribs spring out from the spine and should not be confused with 'barrel-chested'. An oval-chested Greyhound can have well-sprung ribs.

RING TAIL	Tail carried over back almost in a circle.
ROACH	Usually a roached back; an upward-curved backline; a hump over ribs and loin; convex curvature of backline.
ROMAN NOSE	Bridge of nose bends outward; convex curvature of nose.
ROSE EAR	Drop ear (usually small) that folds back and over so as to show the internal folds.
RUDDER	Tail.
RUFF	Long and thick hair growth around the neck; the mane is on top of the neck.
SABRE TAIL	Tail carried like a sabre; semi-circle; German Shepherd Dog tail at rest is carried like a sabre.
SABLE	Black outer hairs over a light-coloured coat. (Usually brown to light brown.)
SADDLE	A dark (usually black) marking over the back; from the location of a saddle as placed on a horse.
SCAPULA	The shoulder blade.
SCISSORS BITE	*See* Bite.
SCREW TAIL	A naturally occurring short tail that twists.
SECOND THIGH	Lower thigh; from stifle to hock joint.
SELF COLOUR	One colour.
SEPTUM	Line between nostrils.
SHALLOW BRISKET	Lack of depth of ribs.
SHORT-BODIED	Short between front of chest and rear of dog.
SHORT-COUPLED	Short space between last rib and pelvis.
SHOULDERS	Shoulder blade and supporting muscles.
SHOULDER HEIGHT	Height of a dog measured from the withers to the ground.
SICKLE-HOCKED	Inability to straighten the hock joint on the back reach of the hind leg; dog moves with a permanent angle in hock joint.
SICKLE TAIL	Tip of tail vertically above root, but tail bent as a semi-circle; tail carried out and up in a semi-circle (shaped like a sickle).
SINEW	A tendon; that which transmits strength of

	power from muscle to bone.
SINEWY	Having sinews, especially of marked development; strong; tough; firm.
SINGLE TRACKING	The tendency of a dog on the move to travel with the paw prints in a nearly straight line.
SLAB-SIDED	Ribs too flat for the given breed of dog; flat ribs with too little spring from the spinal column for the given breed.
SLED DOG	A dog used to pull sleds over snow, usually an Arctic breed.
SMOOTH COAT	A dog with a short, non-curly coat.
SNIPY	Muzzle pointed and weak; no fill under the eyes with narrow thin jaws.
SOUND	Free from flaw, defect or decay; perfect for the kind; undamaged or unimpaired; healthy; robust; not diseased.
SOUNDNESS	A dog is sound or unsound. Soundness refers to health or structural perfection for the breed. A barrel chest would be sound for a Bulldog, unsound for a Greyhound. Unsound is usually equivalent to faulty.
SPECTACLES	Darker or shaded marking around the eyes, as on a Keeshond.
SPLAYED FEET	Toes spread out; open feet; usually with a 'down in the arch'.
SPREAD HOCKS	Hocks pointing outwards; opposite of cow hocks.
SPRING OF RIBS	Spring of the ribs from the backbone; well-sprung ribs have plenty of lung and heart room; well-sprung ribs slant backwards at about 45 degrees to the spine so that when they rotate they increase breathing capacity.
SQUIRREL TAIL	Tail carried up and curved too far forwards.
STANCE	A dog's stance; manner of standing.
STANDARD	The official KC-recognized Breed Standard that describes the ideal dog of the breed.
STAND-OFF COAT	Coat that stands out from the body as on a Pomeranian; stiff hair supported by a dense undercoat creates a stand-off coat.
STERN	Rear end; tail; to the rear.
STENUM	The breast bone; the brisket.
STIFLE	The stifle joint is between the upper and lower thigh; stifle includes the area on each side of the stifle joint. A 'well-bent stifle' has a

	marked angle at the stifle joint.
STILTED	Without bend at the rear leg joints; usually used as a 'stilted gait'; or moving without flexing straight joints.
STOP	The change in profile line between the muzzle and skull; the 'break' between muzzle and skull.
STRAIGHT-HOCKED	Insufficient bend in the hock joint for the breed.
STRAIGHT SHOULDERS	Shoulder blade nearly vertical as opposed to well laid back.
STRIDE	A complete action of one limb prior to repeating the action.
SUBSTANCE	Plenty of bone; refers more to heaviness of bone rather than fat. A well-muscled dog also has substance, but a well-muscled small-boned dog is not referred to as having substance.
SWAYBACK	The back with downward bow in it; concave curvature of back from withers to pelvis.
SYMMETRY	A general term to express a pleasing agreement between all parts of the dog; the head, neck, body, legs and tail form a symmetrical picture; balanced.
TAIL SET	How the base of the tail sets on the rump.
TEAM	More than two dogs, matched in appearance and shown as a team.
TERRIER	A group of dogs, the origin of which was to hunt vermin.
TERRIER FRONT	Straight front, as found on Fox Terriers; a fault in some breeds and desirable in others.
THIGH	In dogs the area from the pelvis to the hock joint; upper thigh is from the pelvis to the stifle; lower thigh is from the stifle to the hock joint.
THROATINESS	Excessive skin under the throat.
TICKED	Small spots of coloured hair on a background colour (usually white background). A pattern that has variable colours.
TOPKNOT	A tuft of hair on top of the head, as on a Poodle.
TOPLINE	Line from withers to tail as seen in silhouette.
TOY DOGS	A group of dogs, small in size.
TRIANGULAR EYE	A somewhat three-cornered appearing eye;

	the tissue surrounding the eye has a triangular shape.
TRICOLOUR	A dog with black, white and tan coat colours.
TRIM	To clip a dog's coat; to shape a coat by removing part of the hair.
TROT	Diagonal support in motion: right front and left rear supporting dog, then left front and right rear.
TUCK-UP	Narrow-waisted in the loin area; rise in bottom line at loin area; ribs are normal (not herring-gutted) and tuck-up begins at the end of the ribs.
TULIP EAR	Named after the tulip petal; ear erect with edges curved forwards along sides.
TURN-UP	Foreface turned up as on a Bulldog; up-tilted foreface; upsweep of underjaw.
TYPE	The characteristic features distinguishing a breed. *See also* p. 105.
UNBALANCED	Parts do not fit one another; not symmetrical. *See also* Symmetry.
UNDERSHOT	The upper jaw does not extend out as far as the lower jaw; lower jaw projects beyond the upper jaw.
UNSOUND	A derogatory remark about a dog which indicates one or a number of faults. *See also* Soundness.
UPPER ARM	The part of the front leg from the elbow to the shoulder blade.
WALLEYE	Eye with whitish iris; associated with merle coat colour in Collies, Shelties and also found with Harlequin Danes.
WEAVING	As the dog travels the free foot is swung round the support foot.
WEEDY	Light-boned.
WHEATEN	Fawn-coloured coat; pale yellow coat.
WHELPS	Unweaned puppies.
WHIP TAIL	Carried straight, stiff and pointed.
WIRE-HAIR	A hard, wiry coat as the Wire-haired Fox Terrier.
WITHERS	The bony projection of vertebrae in the vicinity of the shoulder blades; the highest point of the shoulder below the neck; first eight dorsal vertebrae.
WRINKLE	Wrinkled skin on foreface and forehead as on

	a Basenji or Bloodhound.
WRY-FACED	Upper jaw area of the foreface noticeably out of level.
WRY-JAWED	The lower jaw noticeably out of level or awry.

Useful addresses

The Kennel; Club, 1 Clarges Street, Piccadilly, London WC1Y 8AB
   Tel: 01–493–6651
Canine Studies Institute, London Rd, Bracknell, Berkshire RG12 6QN
   Tel: (0344) 420898
Our Dogs, 5 Oxford Road, Station Approach, Manchester M60 1SX
   Tel: (061 236) 2660
Dog World, 9 Tufton Street, Ashford, Kent TN23 1QN
   Tel: (0233) 22389
PRO-Dogs, 4 New Road, Ditton, Maidstone, Kent M20 6A
   Tel: (0732) 848499

Bibliography

* The Official Breed Standards, The Kennel Club.
* Kennel Club Yearbook.
* *Dogsteps – Illustrated Gait at a Glance*, Rachel Page-Elliott; Howell.
* *The Dog in Action*, McDowell Lyon; Howell (out of print).
* *Take Them Round Please*, Tom Horner; David and Charles.
  Dog Judges Handbook, Sarah Tieljen; Howell.
* *Art and Science of Judging Dogs*, Thelma and Curtis Brown; B & E Publications (out of print).
* *World Encyclopaedia of Dogs*, Ferelith Hamilton; New English Library (out of print).
* *Nicholas Guide to Dog Judging*, Anna Nicholas; Howell.
  All About Mating, Whelping and Weaning, David Cavill; Pelham.
* *New Art of Breeding Better Dogs*, Kyle Onsett; Howell.
  Dogs and How to Breed Them, Hilary Harmer; Gifford.
  Inheritance of Coat Colour in Dogs, Clarence Little; Howell.
  Dog Shows and Show Dogs, Catherine Sutton; K & R Books (out of print).
* *Canine Terminology*, Harold Spira; Harper and Row.
* *Dogs – Breeding and Showing*, Catherine Sutton; Batsford.
* *Canine Locomotion and Gait Analysis*, C. Brown; Hoflin Publishing/ Canine Studies Institute.

* Specially recommended.

Index